Guilden Morden in the 1940's

A Village Pulling Together

Map of the Parish

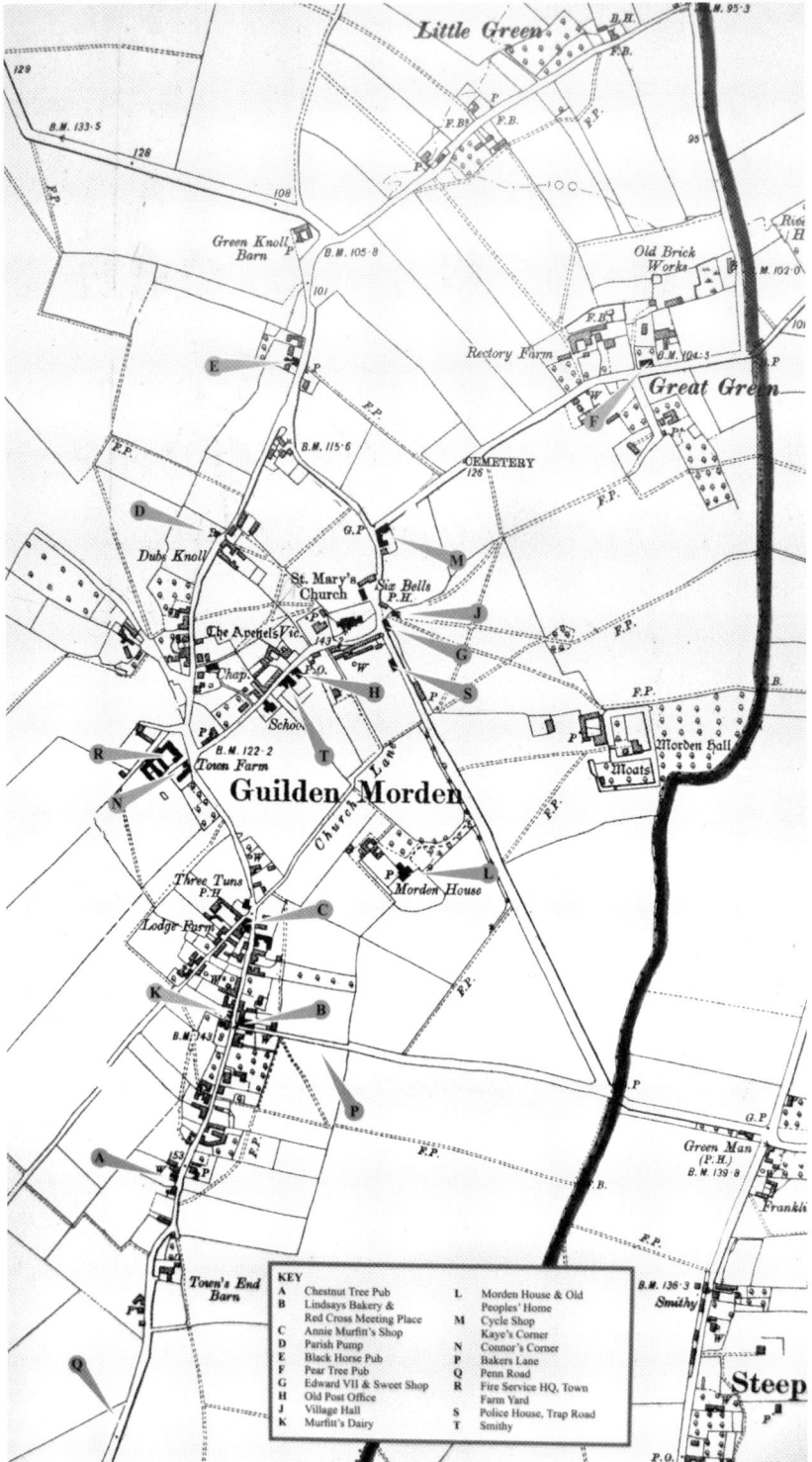

Little Green

B.H.
F.B.

B.M. 133·5

129
128
108

F.P.

Green Knoll Barn
B.M. 105·8

F.B.
F.B.

F.B.

Old Brick Works

M. 102·0

Rectory Farm

B.M. 104·5

Great Green

E

F

B.M. 115·6

CEMETERY
126

F.P.

D

Dubs Knoll

G.P.

M

St. Mary's Church

Six Bells P.H.

J

The Arpels Vic.

G

Chap.

P.O.

H

S

School

P

R

B.M. 122·2
Town Farm

T

Morden Hall

Moats

N

Guilden Morden

Church Lane

Three Tuns P.H.

Morden House

L

Lodge Farm

C

K

B

B.M. 143·8

P

Green Man (P.H.)
B.M. 139·8

A

F.B.

Town's End Barn

B.M. 136·3

Smithy

Q

Steep

P.O.

KEY

A	Chestnut Tree Pub	L	Morden House & Old Peoples' Home
B	Lindsays Bakery & Red Cross Meeting Place	M	Cycle Shop
C	Annie Murfitt's Shop		Kaye's Corner
D	Parish Pump	N	Connor's Corner
E	Black Horse Pub	P	Bakers Lane
F	Pear Tree Pub	Q	Penn Road
G	Edward VII & Sweet Shop	R	Fire Service HQ, Town Farm Yard
H	Old Post Office	S	Police House, Trap Road
J	Village Hall	T	Smithy
K	Murfitt's Dairy		

Guilden Morden in the 1940's

A Village Pulling Together

Edited by Geoff Harper and Graham Dellar

Published 2015
Guilden Morden Local History Group

DEDICATION

This book is dedicated to all Guilden Morden residents and evacuees who lived in the parish during the 1940's.

© Geoffrey Harper and Graham Dellar

First printed 2015

ISBN 978-0-9576147-1-0

Background image on cover © Sir Brian Batsford

Typeset in 10pt Palatino Linotype
Printed and bound by CPI Group (UK) Ltd, Croydon, CR0 4YY

Published by Guilden Morden Local History Group and EAH Press.

The publishers have made every effort to trace the owners of photographs used in this book. In cases where they have been unsuccessful they invite copyright holders to contact them direct.

The Guilden Morden Local History Group is a member of the Cambridgeshire Association for Local History.

Project supported by the Heritage Lottery Fund and sponsored by Guilden Morden Parish Council. A free copy of this book has been offered to each household in Guilden Morden.

heritage lottery fund

LOTTERY FUNDED

Contents

Foreword

Most readers of this book will be too young to remember the 1940's. Those of you who do have memories of those days were children or youngsters at the time. Your recollections are of a less complicated, more self contained village life, overlaid with vivid memories of bomber and fighter aircraft overhead, gas masks and the blackout.

If you do not have those memories you may find it hard to imagine life without mains water or electricity, council refuse collections or television and would be amazed at the possibility of bombs dropping or planes crashing nearby!

When the present incarnation of the Guilden Morden Local History Group was formed in January 2013, it was agreed that our first project would be about Guilden Morden in the 1940's. We are fortunate that some of our members do remember those times and were able to provide their recollections to enliven the research on which we embarked.

We were advised that a grant could be obtained from the Heritage Lottery Fund to enable us carry out our project and involve the community. Our application was successful on the second attempt and we were also fortunate in persuading our Parish Council to sponsor us. In January 2014, with the funds now available, we purchased recording equipment, arranged oral history training and then recorded the memories of some fifteen local people. After conducting research and collecting many photographs and interesting memorabilia, we staged an exhibition in September 2014 at the Congregational Church. With 1940's style refreshments provided by the Church and our members; with the music of the time in the background; and 1940's vehicles on Pound Green, the exhibition was seen by over five hundred visitors.

The final part of our project was to publish this book. It contains most of the detail that we have discovered about our village in the 1940's, illustrated with some fascinating photographs and with appropriate background detail. We hope you will enjoy it. If you remember those times it will bring back the memories; if you don't – we hope you will be intrigued by life in Guilden Morden some seventy years ago.

Acknowledgements

We very much appreciate the help we have received in preparing this book. In addition to the research involved, many people have given their time in contributing their memories of Guilden Morden in the 1940's; in searching for photographs and documents; and by contributing to the content and production of this book. Much of the material in the book has been taken from the displays at the exhibition staged by the Guilden Morden Local History Group in September 2014. Our thanks therefore extend to all those who helped to make that event such a great success.

We must thank in particular The Heritage Lottery Fund and the Guilden Morden Parish Council for funding our project, which has included the recording of residents' memories of the village in the 1940's, the exhibition and the publication of this book. The project would not have succeeded without the expert help and advice so generously given by Marian and Michael Chapman of Fusion Creative Marketing for the exhibition and by Geoff Barlow for the book.

Our thanks are also due to the Royston Museum for their help in facilitating our researching of the Royston Crow archives; to David Crow for his enthusiastic support and the loan of photographs of Steeple Morden and Bassingbourn airfields. Also to Reg Rogerson, who lent us exhibits and photographs. Sadly, Reg passed away earlier this year. Others who generously lent photographs, vehicles and artefacts include Jane Boyd, Chris Jennings, John King, Cicely Murfitt, Ross Nuten, Jean Percival, John Sole, John Stevenson and Christopher Tordoff.

The book includes many extracts from the written and recorded memories of local people. These contributors are listed in Appendix 3. Without their firsthand accounts of life some seventy years ago, our history would be much the poorer. We are indebted to Sarah Baylis, who provided training and support in recording oral history and to Susan Barnard of Academic Transcriptions for transcribing our recordings. We also are indebted to Ken Wells for extracts from his books.

Letters from a fictitious American airman based at Steeple Morden during the war have been written by Jean Warren and are included in Appendix 1. Our thanks are due to her for bringing to life this aspect of our local history. Jean with other members of the Congregational Church and the ladies of the History Group provided much appreciated 1940's style refreshments.

We are grateful to Yvonne Harper and Maureen Popp for their proof reading and constructive comments.

Finally, we would like to thank all the members of our local history group for their contributions to both the exhibition and this book – including Bill and Brenda Davies, John Dellar, Pat Dellar, Christine Furmston, Irene and Ivan Gentle, Barbara and Brian Haines, Doreen Mitchell, Corinne Morley, Maureen Popp, Kathy Tear and Cynthia Worboys.

If we have omitted anyone, please accept our apologies and appreciation.

Geoff Harper and Graham Dellar

Chapter 1

Guilden Morden - An Introduction

As can be seen from the map, Guilden Morden is a long and narrow parish in the South-West of Cambridgeshire. On the western (county) boundary is the River Rhee (the Cam); to the south is the A505, formerly the Baldock-Royston Turnpike and originally the Icknield Way; to the north is the Tadlow Bridge over the Cam; and the east is bounded by the village of Steeple Morden. The land is mainly clay (gault) to the north and chalk further south. This has always been a farming village. The main part of the village is in the north of the parish and combines the long winding High Street and the area around the Church of St. Mary with the outlying areas of Great Green and Little Green. South of the main village there is the farmhouse and settlement of Cold Harbour. To the north-west of the village is Hooks Mill, which was originally a water mill. In the south the parish includes part of the village of Odsey, including Odsey Grange and House.

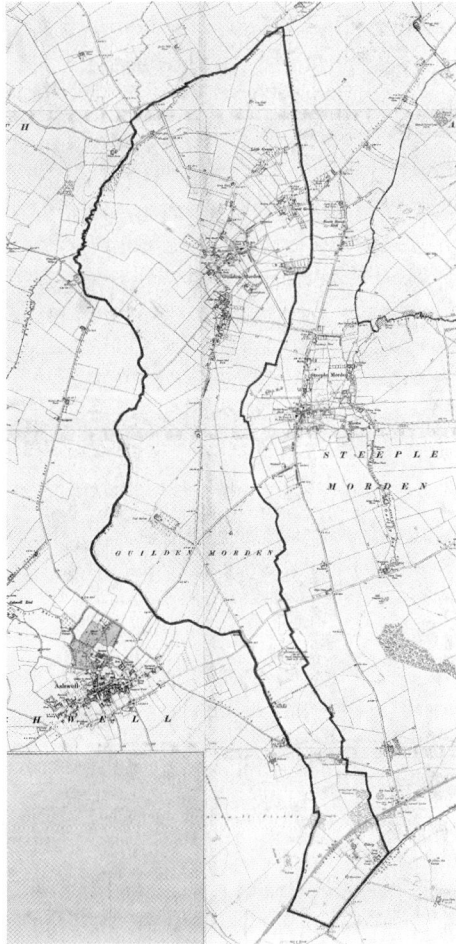

Early History

The area has been settled for more than two thousand years. There are Bronze Age and Iron Age burial sites in the south of the parish and there was a Roman Villa and a large Romano-British cemetery near the Ruddery Spring[1]. The Icknield Way (see above) is one of the oldest roads in Great Britain, existing well before Roman times.

---

[1] The Ruddery Spring is associated with The Ruddery, a track which starts in Ashwell and continues into Guilden Morden Parish and on towards Royston. The Ruddery Spring feeds the Ruddery Brook.

The two Mordens were separated in 1015. The origin of the name 'Guilden' is uncertain but may mean golden (for rich and productive). Morden probably means hill on the moor.

In the Domesday Book, Guilden Morden is named 'Mordune', distinguishing it from Steeple Morden. There were about two hundred and eighty inhabitants at that time. Four people are named to whom land had been given by William the Conqueror. These estates   passed down as five manors – Pichards, Bondesbury, Odsey, Avenels[2] and Foxleys. Manors were the main economic units in those days rather than the village. The Domesday Book mentions a water mill which was part of Pichards Manor. This was almost certainly Hooks Mill.

Medieval History

By 1100, the hamlet of Redreth (or Redderia) was established. This was situated about 2 km from the south of the village and included a chapel. It was last mentioned in the 1340's and may have been deserted due to the Black Death.

Our church of St. Mary was so named by 1472 and is a large and stately building, built of field stones, with a tower and short spire.

At Odsey there was a Cistercian grange.[3] By the 16th century this was no longer owned by the monks and by the 18th century became gentlemen's residences.

In the 14th century agricultural conditions were in a poor state partly due to excessive taxation and much arable land was not cultivated. The population of the village was probably under three hundred in those times.

In the Peasants Revolt of 1381, Morden Hall, a large house surrounded by a moat, was looted and partly destroyed by rioters. The Hall was rebuilt soon afterwards.

The principal crops in the Middle Ages were barley and wheat and substantial numbers of sheep were kept – possibly as many as eight hundred at the end of the 14th century. Before the 17th century saffron was grown in the parish.

19th Century

Enclosure was carried out in 1805, involving 1,922 acres of open fields and commons.

By 1845, five large farms occupied over half the parish – Manor Farm, Town Farm, Cold Harbour Farm, Rectory Farm and the Odsey estate. There were also about ten smaller farms. By 1900 only seven farmers remained. Wheat was the principal crop. Sheep keeping gradually declined.

Most inhabitants of the village were farm labourers. For some, their income was supplemented by the women working at straw plaiting.

There was much poverty during the 19th century. Until 1834, the parish overseer collected rates which were used to provide support for the poor, known as

---

[2] Note that the spelling of 'Avenels' has been standardised throughout.

[3] A 'grange' is an estate used for food production by a monastery.

'outdoor relief'. If the poor refused or were unable to work they could be placed in a workhouse. Guilden Morden had its own workhouse, thought to have been opposite the church. After 1834, parishes were allocated to Poor Law Unions and large workhouses were built in which conditions were designed to be less desirable than those experienced by a labourer of the lowest class. Guilden Morden belonged to the Royston Union.

To escape poverty many sought a better life by emigrating. Unfortunately, for some Guilden Morden people this ended in disaster. In 1845, twenty three villagers were drowned on the voyage to Australia.

In 1840 an independent non conformist congregation opened a chapel in Pound Green. At least half of the villagers of Guilden Morden were chapel-goers at this time.

The village had a number of craftsmen in the mid 19th century, including blacksmiths, a wheelwright, carpenters, shoemakers and tailors.

There was a brick-works near Great Green, which continued to the 1920's.

In 1850, the Great Northern Railway Company built the Hitchin to Royston line, with a station at Odsey.

From the 1860's until the 1880's, the village profited from the coprolite boom. Coprolites are the droppings and fossilized remains of creatures living in the seas and coastal areas during the Cretaceous period. These were mined for fertilizer. At its peak in the 1870's, digging for coprolites employed seventy six men from the village. The industry declined after 1881 and the population of the village reflected this, falling from a peak of one thousand and fifty nine in 1871 to six hundred and forty six in 1901. Another reason for the fall in population was a decline in agriculture.

In 1881, a great fire destroyed some thirteen cottages and barns in the Pound Green area, the flames quickly consuming the thatch and wood.

20th Century

The village experienced more change in the 20th century than in any previous period. In the last decades of the 19th and early 20th century there was a real depression in agriculture. In particular wheat growing declined greatly due to cheaper foreign imports. However, agriculture continued to be a major focus for the village, but now employing a steadily reducing proportion of the local population, due to mechanisation. The population continued to decrease to five hundred or so during the Second World War, but has since increased steadily to more than nine hundred in 2015.

The village housing stock has increased with new developments such as those in Bells Meadow, Cannons Close and Fox Hill Road. There are now less open spaces in the village than there were in the 1940's.

Piped water and an electricity supply came to the village by the 1940's and sewerage by the 1970's. Communications have been transformed with telephone land lines, mobile phones and computers, although connections and speeds often fall short of expectations.

With improved road and rail transport many residents now work outside the village – in Cambridge, London and elsewhere, although more people now run businesses or work from home. Bus services have declined whilst the road traffic through the village has increased greatly.

The village school moved to new premises in Pound Green in 1974, after one hundred and twenty four years in its building in Church Street.

Village crafts have gradually declined since 1914 – the brickfield closed in the 1920's; the watermill (assisted by a windmill and an oil fired engine) closed in the 1930's; and the last blacksmith's closed in the 1960's. Sadly, the number of pubs has also reduced from nine in 1900 to just one today and the village post office closed in 1998.

Land for a village recreation ground was originally purchased in 1912 and this was further extended in 1991.

Chapter 2

Everyday Life of the Village

Although the 1940's are well within living memory, life in the village then was very different to our life now in 2015. Clearly the war had a significant impact on the village, particularly with the proximity of the airfields at Steeple Morden and Bassingbourn. There are also the huge differences in our lives since the 1940's brought about by technological advances and economic growth. Although people in the 1940's were without many of the things that we now take for granted, there is no sense that lives were any less happy or less rewarding – often quite the reverse! Through the voices of those who lived in the village during the 1940's, this chapter illustrates the contrasts between then and now.

"It (Guilden Morden) was a magical place as far as I am concerned. This end of the village anyway, and later today, if you remind me, I will show you a map of the parish of Guilden Morden, and I will show you what was orchards and what was meadows, and you will realise the difference now. It was so different. We would... as kids we would disappear at say ten or eleven o'clock in the morning, with an apple, and maybe a crust in a bit of paper or something like that, and we would go across the meadows and just catch butterflies, look at all the different flowers, scrump a few apples or a few plums out the orchards. Go down to Mobbs Hole....there is a note that we had one of those fuel tanks which they used to eject from the aeroplanes, we cut the top out of it and made it into a canoe, but of course, because it was round, it used to tip over quite easily. So Richard Murfitt and Ron Bowen designed some floats out of other kind of cans, to tie on the side of it, or fix on the side of it, so that it didn't go over quite so easy. But then we took those off one day to go down – as we called it the river – and we went to Hooks Mill, right down the river. We couldn't do that now, because it is overgrown. They talk about cleaning ditches, but it was a river in those days."
John Dellar *(Oral History Recordings)*

"Very different to what it is today. It was mainly the council houses, and the cottages, and one or two big houses, where mainly farmers lived. We didn't have any form of... well, we never had cars, for instance, like there are today. Very few and far between. It was so quiet on the roads in those days, we could have the hopscotch all out on the main road, and all the children from the council houses would come out and play. And then occasionally someone would say, "There's a car coming", and you all went to the sides of the road.
I know we used to sometimes go round to the back of where Miss Murfitt's house and Miss Murfitt's shop was. Murfitt's had a dairy round the back, where they did the milking. And we often used to go round there, and watch the milking, and then wander along. And if it was harvest time we'd perhaps stop in the fields, and get a ride on the trolleys, and then get told off for being late back from school."
Marie Parker *(Oral History Recordings)*

As will be seen from Chapter 5, particularly during the war years, the supply of water and electricity to houses in the village was either not yet in place or in its very early stages. This combined with the absence of appliances such as refrigerators, freezers, washing machines etc. which depend on these supplies, meant that domestic life was very different then. Marjorie Baker, who lived at 4 Avenel Terrace, describes her family's domestic life in detail:

"Well the house was two-up and two-down, as they describe it. The, what shall we say, the privacy was up the garden, in the barn, there was a barn, where you kept your coal and chopped sticks and done all sorts there. It had a very small strip of garden, and of course the toilet and everything was in the barn. It was the... there was no mains sewerage or anything...... And that was quite interesting because there was a certain area in this strip of garden that was surrounded by wire netting with a little gate and it had honeysuckle growing all round it. And there was a washing line along the garden, but in the house the stairs went up out of the kitchen. They had a door on them, and there was two bedrooms, a larger one and the smaller one, and you could get a double bed and a single bed in the front bedroom, they were quite large. And the back bedroom had a double bed in it. And you had room for a wardrobe, and mother was very particular. The dressing table was near the window and the chest-of-drawers and all the usual mod cons we needed. And the next thing was downstairs the kitchen had what they call an old gypsy fireplace in it which consisted of two pillars of brick with some iron, what shall we say, iron bars across it, and on there you could balance a broiler, a small boiler, which you boiled your washing in on a Monday. You lit the fire under these bars and that all... and of course the smoke went up the chimney as it does normally. But the other thing was in the kitchen there was an old stone sink, not even a white sink, it was stone, it was brown stone, it was... and there was no running water, you fetched your water from a pump on the end of the terrace. And there were drains from the sink outside, so that wasn't too bad, you could put your waste water down there. Anyway, there was a pantry under the stairs and on Good Fridays this pantry used to be cleared and white-washed, because that was how it was kept clean. It had an old stone floor and in the summer they had a bucket of water in there where we kept our milk cool, and we could also make jellies because jellies set on the cold stone floor, in the basin on the cold stone floor. And there were shelves where you kept all your tins and plates and so on and so forth and some hooks to hang your cups on. And there was a safe. Now a safe was a wooden container with mesh sides and front, and this is where you put the fresh meat, and all the meat and all the perishable goods to keep the flies off them I suppose really. And that is how we were. There was lots of tins because... and a bread bin, an enamel type bread bin, the old ones you see nowadays that's being collectables. And also there was one for flour and one for sugar, so that was three. So that was the recollection of what was in the pantry. And of course the saucepans, they were on the bottom shelf as well, there were some saucepans. And these saucepans interestingly enough were always very black, sooty on the outside, because in the living room you had what was known as a kitchen range, and that was a fire that had to be made up with coal, and that (had) an oven with it and that is where you done your cooking and cooked your vegetables and so on. But in the summer time mother purchased an oil burner stove, and it was quite interesting. It had a, it was on a sort of stand, and it had a glass container in the middle where you put the paraffin oil in and it

had an oven built on the top and it had two burners, looked almost like gas burners, and you lit them with a wick coming up through the middle, you see, you turned them up and down like you do an oil lamp. Anyway, so that is what we used to use in the summer rather than have the range alight. But getting back to the saucepans, they were all black because they used to have to be put on the stove and boiled and used to cook your vegetables or whatever you wanted to do, you know. But the interesting thing on that was as well you could put a rice pudding in there or a casserole or whatever and just forget about it, so long as you kept the fire made up. So that meant in the kitchen you had what was called a coal scuttle, and that was usually a metal container or something, we used a galvanised bucket with coal in, which you had to go up the garden to the barn to fill up. So that was a ritual that used to have to be done every night.

Now with regard to fresh drinking water and so on, you had a galvanised bucket, and that had a wooden lid on top of it. And you used to fill it up from the pump, and that was what we used for drinking water. On wash days it was quite interesting because the old galvanised bath came in and went on the kitchen table. Now the kitchen table was, underneath, a mangle, and it folded down and had a wooden top on it, so during the week it was a wooden table but on wash day it became a mangle. So you had extra buckets and so on of water to do your washing with, and a big... which I recollect us being bathed in one on occasion... you had a nice sort of, not aluminium, an enamel bath, a white one with a red rim round it. And that is where they put the rinsing water to rinse the washing, and that. But all the washing was done by hand, apart from what we boiled on gypsy grate.

In the early days we didn't have electricity, we had a lamp on the table, or candles or another oil lamp in the kitchen. But always when I was sort of small it was, 'Mind the lamp' was the slogan that used to come out very often, you know, when you were sort of playing and things like that. I had a small chair that was given to me, I don't know where it came from actually, but it was a small child's chair and with a nice little leather seat in it, like a little armchair affair, and I kept that for years. But eventually that got woodworm so that went out. But I had this little chair and that used to be in the corner and I used to sit in that and read my books. And I had a sort of a toy box that was a wooden box. I think my father may have made it, because he liked to do a bit of woodwork, and I kept certain toys and books and things in there. But all my big books, I used to get an annual at Christmas and, or a girl's book, Girl's Own, or something like that, I can't just remember. But they used to be kept upstairs, you'd keep them upstairs. And I had a couple of nice dolls that were, now I realise, collector's items, and what happened to them I've no idea, but they were German-made, lovely dolls, all ready dressed and so they were kept upstairs as well. And I had a nice doll's pram, which was big enough, or made well enough to put... I think you could almost have put a baby in it, because it was so well made with its mattresses and, you know, everything properly, like a proper baby carriage. Anyway, that was kept upstairs as well, so here we go. So that was memories of that.

I think Friday night was quite exciting really. It was bath night, so in come the galvanised bath again and the water was warmed up on the old gypsy stove in the boiler, and of course I had a bath and everything else. Well of course I got sent to bed so what happened after then, I presume my parents must have had a so-called bath or whatever, I don't know about all that.

Most people grew a lot of things in their garden. A slogan was 'Dig for Victory'. We ourselves were lucky, my grandad kept chickens and had all kinds of fruit, plums, red, white and blackcurrants, blackberries, apples, pears and he kept bees, so we had good food. Lemonade drink was a favourite, lemon crystals made up and then diluted. Tizer was another favourite. The village shop sold about everything so again we were very lucky. In town when there was a special allocation of some special food, queues formed for hours. It became a good British institution. And another thing comes to mind re food, we always had the Sunday School treats, one at Christmas in the village hall, complete with conjurer - Mr Newton Hunt with the rabbit in the hat. Packets of Smith's Crisps were obtainable at the Edward VII. Mr Steele the landlord would serve us at the back door. He also did the village paper round on his bike. We used to get fresh fish from Crump's butchers plus the meat, so it was good. Mac Fisheries shop in Hitchin sold fresh salmon and that was a real treat. For tea, tinned salmon was a luxury too as was tinned fruit, all scarce."

Marjorie Baker *(Oral History Recordings)*

Barbara Haines, who lived in Phoenix Row (Fox Hill Road) has her own vivid memories, which also illustrate how things have changed over the last seventy years.

"Our house was a two-up two-down, the wash house outside had a copper which was lit for a bath once a week and for boiling clothes on wash day. The bath was a long tin one and the wash tubs were smaller. After the wash the clothes went through a mangle. We had a well in the garden which was used by all the tenants in the row of cottages until we had a tap placed in the centre of the row for us all to use. Our toilet was of course outside next to the wash house. I remember there was no light in there and it was a long way down to the actual toilet and the only way you knew you were there was when you kicked it."

During the 1940's I was lucky and had a bike. My friend didn't have one and her and I used to go down to Wendy to visit my Gran and Grandad. We would take it in turns to ride from one telephone pole to the next while the other one walked to pick it up, and continue this all the way to Wendy where my Gran always had an apple dumpling boiling in the grate. During our latter school years when it was potato picking time we had about two weeks off school to pick up potatoes for Farmer George Barnes who farmed round North Brook End. We also went pea picking but this was in the school holidays.

During these years we left Guilden Morden School at fourteen and then went to Bassingbourn old school for our last year. We travelled from Guilden Morden on Gentle's Coaches which came from Ashwell, then from here to Wrestlingworth crossroads, then to Croydon, then to Wendy and Shingay on to North End, Bassingbourn."

Barbara Haines *(Written Memories)*

All the people that recorded their memories of Guilden Morden have happy memories of the 1940's, although of course most were children or teenagers at the time. Albert Willmott was married to Lily during the 1940's.

"But life was good ....we didn't have much, but what we did have we enjoyed.....I think they were lovely years. I prefer life then to what I see now"

Albert Willmott *(Oral History Recordings)*

Chapter 3

Guilden Morden Parish Council

Guilden Morden Parish Council was established following the Local Government Act of 1894, which created Parish Councils. The first Chairman was Mr. H.G. Fordham J.P., who said he was anxious to make his own parish *"a model of completeness"*. The first lady Councillor was elected in 1895. Amongst the first acts of the new Parish Council was to provide allotments and to purchase a Burial Ground from the Wimpole Estate for £60.

The following are extracts from the minutes of the Parish Council from 1939 to 1949: Note that all meetings were held in the (old) school.

1939 - A joint meeting with the Air Raid Wardens was held in September 1939. At the meeting it was agreed that the Parish Council were to supply hose pipe and sand, but a public water supply not being available, until the question of fire fighting became a matter for the District Council.

The Clerk's position was offered to Mr. Oswald Kaye. He accepted and resigned from the Council. A £50 bond was required.[1] He remained the Clerk throughout the 1940s and he did not relinquish the post until 1973.

It was recorded that Mr. W.G. Dellar was Chief Air Raid Warden.

A resolution was passed expressing dissatisfaction with the education facilities in the area. The 'Ashwell Scheme' should have been open to the parish.

1940 - The village hall was nominated as a secure room for people made homeless by an air raid.

The Cambridge Federation of Women's Institutes wrote asking for help in the collection of surplus vegetables. The Council replied that they were willing to help, but didn't think there would be any.

The schoolroom was insufficiently blacked out. The meeting was therefore held in Headmistress, Miss Pullen's room.

The Council was asked to take steps to get a telephone installed in the home of the Chief Air Raid Warden. (Later it was reported to have been installed).

1941 - It was reported that Mr. Steel, the licensee of the Edward VII, had ignored an instruction concerning his poultry. The Clerk was therefore instructed to write to the Ashwell Brewery Co. (a previous minute noted that poultry, belonging to Mr. Steel had been straying onto the Recreation Ground). A letter had later been received from Russell Fordham in reply to the letter sent to Ashwell Brewery Co. It was said to be 'A spiteful and sarcastic reply'. The Clerk was to write a further

---

[1] Note that professional Parish Clerks were not appointed at this time, as they are now. Mr Kaye was the village blacksmith.

letter to Mr Steel. If no action resulted, then he was to consult with Mr. Banham of Royston (solicitors).

The Clerk was to use his discretion concerning the digging of deep graves to hold two bodies for the burial of evacuees from Morden House, a home for 'aged invalids'. Too much space was being taken up in the graveyard.

Nominations were put forward for Production Officers for the Cambridgeshire Garden Produce Committee:

Mr. W. Thompson – Avenel Terrace

Mr. A. Worboys – Pound Green

Mr. W. Southgate – Pound Green

Mrs. Fairchild – The Avenels

1942 - Mr Steel's poultry were again reported to be on the recreation ground. The Clerk to write a final letter to Mr. Steel.

The gravedigger was to be paid 10/- (50p) for ordinary graves and £1 for a deep grave.

A letter was to be sent to the Cambridgeshire Education Authority about the state of the school playground.

Mr Lindsay asked if the recreation ground should be ploughed up during the war. This was not agreed but it was agreed that it should be harrowed and rolled and poultry to be kept off. Mr. Frank Murfitt undertook to try to get a flock of sheep to graze it.

A letter of sympathy was to be sent to Cllr. Rayner concerning the tragic death of his son.

1943 - A solicitor's letter had been sent to Mr. Steel. However, the nuisance had ceased for the time being.

Mr. J.D. Thompson of Morden House asked if he could graze animals on the recreation ground. This was agreed, provided that it was still available for games. (Mr. Thompson was charged £4 for the season).

It was reported that no repairs had been carried out to the school playground. The Vicar was to be asked if gravel & cement could be used. A complaint was made about the state of the blackout at the schoolroom. It was decided to speak to the Vicar about it.

Cllr. Murfitt asked for sites for house building after the war. Sites on New Road and Fox Hill owned by Mr. Gilchrist were for sale and these would be the first recommendation. At least six houses were required in addition to those scheduled for replacement.

Cllr. Murfitt (who was a South Cambridgeshire Rural District Councillor) gave information about steps being taken to improve the water supply as there were many complaints about the taste and smell of the water.

It was agreed to obtain a quotation from F. Worboys & Sons for the supply of water to the recreation ground.

It was proposed that the clerk should write to the County Surveyor to ask that roads be marked with white centre lines, especially the road to Ashwell Station. (The County Surveyor later declined to accede to this request).

1944 - A letter was received from Mrs. Rayner complaining about the state of the Morden House Nursing Home. The Clerk was asked to write to the County Council.

Mr. Dellar complained about the quantity of tins, glass etc. dumped in Buxtons Lane. The Clerk was to write to the County Council.

There was again a complaint about the state of the school playground.

The Clerk was to ask the WVS concerning the removal of the rubbish dump (old tins etc.) as these were no longer wanted for salvage.

It was noted that there was an absence of a danger sign at Green Knoll Corner – the County Council was to be informed.

1945 - A letter had been sent by Mr. H. Dellar to the County Council complaining of the state of education at the school due to a shortage of teachers. A reply was made to Mr. Dellar that the Education Committee was prepared to take 'senior children' to Bassingbourn School. The Clerk was then asked to write to the Education Secretary stating that this would not be acceptable unless transport was provided. Later, at the Parish AGM the Council were asked if the school could be taken over from the Church and put under the control of the County Council.

The Burial Ground Caretaker and Gravedigger (Mr. W.A. Dellar) was given one month's notice and asked to continue until 31 March, when he would have achieved twenty one years service.

Dumps of old tins on the recreation ground and in the High Street had been brought to the attention of South Cambridgeshire Rural District Council (SCRDC), who should bear the cost of removal.

The water supply had been connected to the Burial Ground and the Recreation Ground.

Mr. Charles Murfitt resigned after fifty years service. (Mr. Murfitt was the first Clerk to the Council and later Councillor and Chairman).

The Clerk had helped to dig a grave and reported that 15/- (75p) was not enough for the job. It was agreed to increase this to 25/- (£1.50) (£2 for a deep grave).

The Clerk was to write to SCRDC to ask if there is to be a scheme to collect and dispose of un-burnable rubbish.

Cllr. Murfitt reported that housing had been requested under the '3rd Year after the War' programme. Six houses were recommended.

The Reverend Gardiner, the new vicar, reported that the Church of England half of the burial ground had not been consecrated. No objection was raised to it being consecrated.

1946 - Cllr. Lindsey proposed a local dump for rubbish. This would be cheaper than a collection by SCRDC. A dump was to be found.

Proposed that the County Council be asked to kerb the roadside and pave the entrance to the recreation ground.

A letter was received from the vicar to ask if the Bishop of Ely could be asked to consecrate the Church of England part of Burial Ground. This was not agreed as it might give control to the Church – further information was required. Later it was agreed that the burial ground could be consecrated subject to checks being carried out with the Home Office. (It was consecrated on 14 May 1947).

The Vicar was to be asked to hand over the school to the County Council.

The Clerk was to obtain names of the war dead concerning the County War Memorial. (L. Webb's name was put forward).

Enquiries are to be made to the Bedfordshire, Cambridgeshire & Huntingdonshire Electricity Co. concerning the possibility of lighting the village streets.

It was reported that The Victory Celebration Committee had arranged a bonfire on the recreation ground (this took place in June 1945).

A meeting was to be called re the future of the school with the Vicar in attendance.

It was agreed that the British Legion inscribe Second World War names on the War Memorial.

The Clerk was to write to the Eastern National Bus Co. and the Education Secretary concerning a better bus service to Cambridge, especially for schoolchildren.

The problem of Fordham Brewery vehicles driving onto the recreation ground was raised. The Clerk was to write to the Brewery and to complain to Mr Steel about him keeping ducks and feeding them on the recreation ground.

1947 - A letter was to be sent to the Bedfordshire, Cambridgeshire & Huntingdonshire Electricity Company enquiring when the electricity supply would be extended to Great Green.

A letter was to be sent to the Education Secretary concerning the state of the playground and the lack of an assistant teacher.

On the centenary of the school, the Parish Council sent the following message: *"we were very grateful for what had been done in the past and wish that more could be done for those attending the school"*.

It was agreed that the recreation ground be readied for football in the coming season.

The County Surveyor is to be asked to provide 30 mph signs on all approaches and white central lines on roads.

1948 - The Tennis Club asked permission to erect a wire fence around the tennis court on the recreation ground.

The meeting appreciated the collection of un-burnable rubbish and would like another one. This had been agreed to be a twice yearly collection.

30 mph signs have been refused by the Highways Authority.

A complaint received concerning Mr. Steel's erection of a wire fence beyond his boundary and old tins and rubbish thrown onto the ground by him. The Clerk was to write to him.

A discussion took place about handing over the Parish Churchyard to the Council for upkeep and maintenance. It was agreed to insure against claims for damage to boundary fences. No further decision was made awaiting the new vicar.

A Plan was shown for building eight additional houses (no location mentioned).

1949 - The Cricket Club asked for a concrete pitch for practice. This was agreed.

A resolution was passed to bring the following to the attention of the County Council. *'This meeting deplores the action of Messrs. Saul Ltd. in ploughing up the 40' highway known as Cobbs Way and that they restore it to its former condition.'*

A letter was to be written to Mr. Steel concerning him burning hedge trimmings on the recreation ground.

The Precept
The annual precept (i.e. the rates for the village) in the late 1940's were typically £35p.a., being £20 for the burial ground and £15 for general purposes.

The Parish Council in the 1940's

Chairman	Mr Charles Murfitt - Farmer (1901-1945)
	(Charles Murfitt was the First Clerk, and Chairman until 1945)
Parish Clerk	Mr. Oswald Kaye - Blacksmith (1928-1973)
	(Mr Kaye was Clerk from 1939 until 1973)
Councillors:	William Frederick Connor - Farmer (1928-1945)
	Harry Day – Postmaster (1936-1949)
	Harry Charles Dellar – Agricultural Worker (1945-1968))
	William George Dellar – Farmer (1931-1952)
	William James Gentle – Smallholder (1924-1955)
	Alec Jennings (Farmer (1942-1944)
	Sidney Lindsay – Baker & Confectioner (1945-1968)
	Frank Murfitt – Farmer (1920-1962)
	Frank Rayner – Agricultural Worker (1934-1949)
	Stanley Rule - (1934-1949)
	Henry Stanley Rule – Fruit Grower (1946-1952)
	Thomas Wright - Wheelwright (1904-1941)

Chapter 4

Church and Chapel

Guilden Morden Parish Church History

(Source: the Royston Crow 7th September 1951)

The church's roots extend as far back as the reign of William the Conquerer, when Picot, a wealthy Cambridgeshire Sheriff, founded a Canonry at St. Giles Church in Cambridge in the year 1092. Hugolina, the wife of Earl Picot, fell seriously ill, and promised that if she should regain her health, she would dedicate a monastery to St. Giles (her patron saint) and entreat her husband to carry out the vow. The lady recovered quickly, and after consultation with Anselm, Archbishop of Canterbury and Remigius, Bishop of Lincoln, there was founded a Church and offices sufficient for that time in honour of Saint Giles, for six Canons regular near the castle of Cambridge.....They conferred upon these canons the patronage of Churches belonging to them within the confines of the province . . .

The foundation became the Priory of Barnwell, and the patronage of the Living of Guilden Morden continued in the hands of the monks of Barnwell from this date until the dissolution of the Monastery in the year 1589. The patronage was then obtained for Jesus College, Cambridge, by Thirlby, Bishop of Ely.

The Land and Property is mentioned in the Domesday Book, where it is described as in the possession of Picot and other noblemen. Abington Pigotts, incidentally, is said to derive its name from Picot.

Much of the building is local 'clunch', but the tower is a very fine example of the Perpendicular, sixty feet in height. The surmounting spire is of a later date. Its lead bears the Avenels House Arms, which would place its erection at about 1680.

There are six arches on each side of the Nave. The three Early English near the pulpit probably date to 1100-1175, while the others are Early Decorated (1250-1325). The windows of the aisles are all late Perpendicular insertions in older walls. The Chancel is late Perpendicular (1425-1525). The basin of the font is Norman (1100-1175), but the shafts on which it is built are later additions.

The church registers go back to 1653 and the list of Vicars to 1349, when Adath, Seth de Ashwell officiated.

Rare Double Rood Screen

Described by Parker as *"One of the finest Decorated examples extant,"* the double rood screen is an outstanding feature of this church. It is said that there are not more than five others resembling it in the whole of England. According to some authorities, the enclosure on each side formed a small chapel, over which the choir used to sit. The monkish Latin Rhymes painted on the screen are translated in Conybeare's 'Rides round Cambridge' as -

'Jesu, in death's dark hour be thou my friend,
My life to come make sure at this life's end.
Grant me confession, Lord, before I die,
And guide my parting soul to realms on high.'

When the Church was restored during the latter part of the Crimean War, orders were given for the Screen to be pulled down. It was saved through the personal intervention of Mr. Chapman, then living in the Avenels, who appealed to the Earl of Hardwick, owner of the pews within the screen.

Spelling in the Middle Ages

A slab on the Chancel floor bears the inscription: *'Heare lyeth ye body of Mrs. Frances Story who dyed ye 11th day of December 1675,'* The mason, apparently, was unsure of his letter formation, for an upright stroke is carved on both sides of the 'b' and 'd' in body. Another slab indicates that the lady's husband, Thomas Story, predeceased her by five years, and that he invoked a curse on anyone who should *'remove his bones'*. A third slab nearby is in memory of their daughter, Valana Story, who died in February, 1723. It was this family which presented the Church with its silver communion vessels. A Chalice, given by Frances Story, is dated 1666 - the time of the Great Fire of London - and a plate given by the daughter is inscribed with the interesting variation 'Gilded Morden Church.'

Inscription on Vestry Walls

On the walls of the vestry appear some Latin lines, scratched by 16th and 17th century Vicars. Richard Midgley wrote in 1642, *'I will go to Thee, wheresoever Thou callest, most sweet Jesus.'* In 1640 Robert Brides wrote: *'If you know Christ it matters nothing if you are ignorant of all things else.'* and in 1642 he added: *'If you are ignorant of Christ it avails nothing if you know all things else.'* Earlier, John Knightley (Vicar in 1575) wrote: *'Praye for the soule of John Knightley. Vicar of this Parrysh.'* Also in the vestry is a large Crusader's collecting chest, which suggests that collections were then made in kind, and that after sale, the resulting money was sent to the Crusaders.

Recalling 'Hobson's Choice'

A memorial in the corner of the northern aisle was erected by Dame Dorothy Clarke to the memory of her first husband. This lady was the daughter of Thomas

Hobson, the subject of two early epitaphs by Milton, and a Cambridge man commemorated forever in the expression 'Hobson's Choice'.

The Clock in the tower has one hand, as was customary at the time of its erection (1749). It is a twenty four hour clock, which necessitates daily winding, and the steps up to it are dangerously worn. When Mr J. Course carried out repairs some years ago, he also contrived a device whereby the clock could be wound from the floor of the Church. There are six bells, bearing makers names from 1621 to 1708. One ancient bell, undated, bears the Latin inscription *'Blessed be the name of the Lord.'*

Guilden Morden Church Bellringers
(The following information was provided by Mrs. Boyd from the Annual Reports of the Ely Diocesan Association of Church Bell Ringers).
If there were any ringers at Guilden Morden in the 1940's none of them were EDA members. In 1936 there were R. Bedford, P. Dellar, A. Harris, V. Leonard, Rev. Ll.G.S. Price and S. Turnell. None were recorded from 1937 until the 1954 report - D. Kaye, T. Leonard, A. Mynott, P. Turnell and C. Pettengell were listed. In 1955 V. Leonard was added and D. Kaye became O. Kaye. This band continued until 1959 when K. Dellar, C. Bird and F.W. Bird were added.

On 30th June 1940 an order was given out on the wireless that church and chapel bells could only be rung for air raids. On 28th March 1943 the government lifted the ban on ringing which could start again on Easter Sunday 25th April 1943.

There is still an enthusiastic team of bellringers.

Re-dedication of the Bells at St Mary's Church - Sunday 23rd May 1948
(Source: the Royston Crow on 28th May 1948)
In spite of pouring rain a very large congregation was present in the Parish Church on Sunday afternoon for the re-dedication of the bells, which have been restored.
The service commenced with the singing of the Ringers Hymn 'Unchanging God, who livest.' followed by the exhortation read by the Vicar, the Rev. A.F. Gardiner. The lesson was read by the Rev. H.F. Hawkes, followed by the hymn 'Praise my soul the king of heaven.' The Venerable Archdeacon of Ely, H.F. Kirkpatrick, gave an address. During the chanting of Psalm 150, the Archdeacon accompanied by the Vicar, Church Wardens (Mr W.F. Connor and Mr F. Carter), the Rev. H.F. Hawkes and the master bell founder proceeded to the tower. After a short prayer the master bell founder handed the rope of the tenor bell to the vicar's warden, who in turn handed it to the Archdeacon, requesting him to re-dedicate the bells to the glory of God and the use of His Church, following the prayer of dedication the rope was then handed to the vicar with the words, *"Receive these bells, that have been solemnly set apart from profane and unhallowed uses, as a sacred trust committed unto thee, as the appointed Minister of Christ in this Church, and take care that they be only and ever used in God's service and for His Glory."*

A short peal was then rung by members of the Ely Diocesan Change Ringers Association. After prayers by the Archdeacon the service closed with the hymn *'Now thank we all our God'*, and a further peal of bells.

The Clergy, church wardens, ringers and other friends were entertained to tea at the Vicarage by the Vicar and Deaconess. The bells were rung again in the evening by the visiting and local ringers. The work of restoration, which was made possible by the proceeds of the fete and sports meeting, held on August Bank Holiday, 1946, was carried out by Messrs. Mears and Stainbank of Whitechapel.

The fourth, fifth and tenor bells were re-hung on ball bearings, the old crossed pulleys having been discarded, making the whole peal much easier to ring.

St Mary's Sunday School

"St Mary's Sunday School met in the vicarage and they went into church once a month. The teachers were Miss Dorothy Price, the vicar's daughter, followed by Deaconess Gardiner, the sister of the next vicar."
Cynthia Worboys (Oral History Recordings)

"We always went whether we wanted to or not. You'd got to go"
Derek Dellar (Oral History Recordings)

"I was sent to the chapel and I refused to go in and shouted and screamed at my Dad.....after three or four months I suddenly said I wanted to go to church Sunday School and Muriel and Jessica (Dellar) were going and I went with them and I went in."
John Dellar *(Oral History Recordings)*

The children had an annual Treat with a tea party and games on Connor's Meadow, the field behind the school where children regularly played. The Sunday School outing was a big village event when parents and children travelled by coach to the seaside. When this occurred on a weekday, some school staff complained about the loss of school time.

St Mary's Mothers' Union

The annual membership averaged twenty two ladies during the 1940's and meetings were held in the 'Parish Room' in the Vicarage. They met about once a month for services or talks from visiting speakers. Topics ranged from Family Life, Moral Welfare, Prayer and Missionary work. The subscription was 1/6d (7.5p) and the magazine cost 8d (3p). A Deanery Festival, with all the local parishes, was held every year and in 1946 it was held at St Mary's, with The Bishop of Ely giving an address. Earlier that year the Mothers' Union banner had been consecrated and this banner still hangs in church. After the war they knitted woollen squares for blankets for Overseas Missions.

Guilden Morden Congregational Church History
(extract from the Mordens Women's Institute Scrapbook of 1957)

'The building of the Congregational Church was started in 1838 and the opening ceremony was held on the 1st December 1840, when it was said that some twelve to fifteen hundred people were present. Before the opening of this, the present, building, the services were held in the first Independent Chapel which was situated at the back of Lindsay's Bakery and has now been converted into cottages. The first Pastor was the Reverend J, Stockbridge. He was immensely popular, and in 1889 he was presented with a purse containing £317.9s.4d. to mark forty-eight years' ministry at Guilden Morden. He eventually completed fifty years. In 1992 a Congregational Sunday School was added to the building.....'

What is Congregationalism? - The Tradition and History
(Source: The Guilden Morden Parish website)

The Chapel tradition began with men and women taking religion both seriously and with conviction. The seriousness is seen by the actions of Francis Holcroft, Fellow of Clare college, who seeing that the preacher to Litlington was so often too drunk to take the services on Sunday morning, rode out himself from Cambridge to Litlington parish church. Later Holcroft became vicar of Bassingbourn, but in 1662 under the Act of Uniformity, he refused to be held exclusively to the Book of Common Prayer and holding to his convictions was ejected from the living.

Guilden Morden

In Guilden Morden the first record of a dissenting meeting was in 1700 when Thos. Meade applied to the Bishop's Court to register his house as a Meeting House for Presbyterians. This man, Meade, was probably the same Thos. Meade who was fined, with his wife, for keeping a child unbaptised in 1686. The 1674 Hearth Tax lists only a John Meade (with one hearth) in Guilden Morden, possibly the father. The Episcopal Returns of 1669 in fact note no dissenters in Guilden Morden.

However, in nearby Edworth of the nine householders listed under the same Hearth Tax, five were dissenters making a total of twenty dissenters in Edworth - of the 'meanest sort'. They were Independents (that is either Baptists or Congregationalists) and obviously influenced by John Bunyan who used to stop by on his way to Gamlingay. They were described as Anabaptists at Edworth and one, Vaux was 'a prisonr in Hertf. goale' for his pains. The truth might lie in between. The nice people of Wendy might have had a sneaky conventicle or two while Sir

Thos. was out hunting and the poor people of Edworth might have just been ordinary village Anglicans merely wanting a livelier service.

The Compton Census of 1676 lists Guilden Morden with five dissenters which according to J Curtis was 2.3% of the village population. (Melbourn and Meldreth had 18% and Bassingbourn 6.5%.) So the dissenting tradition was not strong.

The present Chapel has the date of 1870 in brick work, but this is merely the date of the frontage. The Chapel was built 1840 on land given by a Mr Leete, then living in the Avenels and called its first minister Joseph Stockbridge in 1840/1, from Homerton College. Teaching areas and vestry were soon added. The frontage of the Chapel was added in 1870. The Hall (called the Schoolroom) was built in 1900. One of the foundation stones was laid by Principal Horobin of Homerton New College. The Manse was completed in 1989, after the Old Manse was sold. A Communion Table presented in 1900 by the Reavell family honours their parents who it was said formed the church from 'a small band of Christians in about 1832'. During the 19th century both church and chapel flourished. Both took an active interest in education for children and adults and both provided schools, the British and National schools respectively, until the 1870 Education Act laid the responsibility on the parish and county councils.

Joseph Stockbridge

Joseph Stockbridge ministered all his life in Guilden Morden, dying in 1892. He is listed as a gentleman in the Kelly's directories and eventually supplied his own house (and possibly stipend). Later in life he was forced to sell his house to the chapel for £400. The house then became the manse until this too was sold by the Chapel in 1987. Since then a new manse has been built on the chapel site and the old schoolroom (built 1900) extensively renovated. In 1972, the churches in the Congregational Union of England and Wales and the English Presbyterian Church were asked to form a new Church, the United Reformed Church. The main practical difference in this union being that the chapel and manse properties would no longer be legally held by the local congregation but by the URC who would also have authority to close and sell the church buildings as well as to appoint ministers. This led to Guilden Morden Congregational Church (and Litlington) declining to join and to remain unaffiliated. Both are now member churches of the Congregational Federation of continuing congregational churches.

Baptisms

14th April 1940 - Donald McNair Jennings
Son of Alec and Janet Jennings of 'Rectory Farm', born 17th February 1940.
27th October 1940 - David Pond
Son of Frederick and Elsie Pond of 'Robindale', born 6th October 1940.

11th May 1941 - Margaret Joan Trafford Clegg
Daughter of John and Lilian Clegg, born 20th November 1933.

11th May 1941 - Anthony Edward Bell
Son of Edward and Doris Bell, born 23 Aug 1937

11th May 1941 - Christopher James Bell
Son of Edward and Doris Bell, born 15 July 1939

27th July 1941 - Lindsay Margaret Lindsay
Daughter of Sidney and Marian Lindsay of *'Balcarres'*, born 28th Aug 1940.

21st December 1941 - Rita Watson
Daughter of Cliff and Kate Watson of *'The Red Barns'*, born 8th Oct 1941.

28th December 1941 - Michael John Harrington
Son of Jack and Lilian Harrington of Ashwell Road, born 5th Nov 1941.

29th March 1942 - Dorothy Christine Jennings
Daughter of Alec and Janet Jennings of *'Rectory Farm'*, born 3rd Feb 1942.

3rd May 1942 - Thomas Williams
Son of Reg and Ellen Williams of *'The Diggings'*, born 24th Feb 1942.

4th July 1942 - Carole Angela Pearce
Daughter of Claude and Kath Pearce of Norfolk, born 17th May 1942.

18th July 1942 - Michael George Izzard
Son of Cyril and Emily Izzard of *'Avenel Terrace'*, born 7th Nov 1941.

2nd August 1942 - Doreen Joan Covington
Daughter of Jack and Edna Covington of Church Street, born 30th Jun 1942.

23rd August 1942 - Alec Raymond Thompson
Son of Bert and Dorothy Thompson of North Brook End, born 12th Jun 1942.

13th September 1942 - Diana Mary Crow
Daughter of Charles and Phillis Crow of Station Road, born 4th July 1942.

14th October 1942 - Arthur Ivan Harris
Son of William and Edith Harris of *'Church Terrace'*, born 28th Aug 1942.

14th March 1943 - June Colley
Daughter of Frank and Elsie Colley of Pound Green, born 1st Feb 1943.

23rd May 1943 - Valerie Mary Cornwall
Daughter of Albert and Rosetta Cornwall of *'Fair View'*, born 13th Feb 1943.

23rd July 1943 - Roy Henry Hart
Son of Harry and Joyce Hart of Silver Street, born 30th Sep 1942.

15th August 1943 - David William Mynott
Son of Alf and Phyllis Mynott of Wendy Road, born 9th Jul 1943.

10th September 1943 - Daphne Eileen Worboys
Daughter of Sid and Gladys Worboys of *'The Dene'*, born 8th Jul 1943.

31st October 1943 - Rosemary Merrill
Daughter of William and Eva Merrill of Brook End, born 12th Sep 1943.

21st November 1943 - Christopher Alec Jennings
Son of Alec and Janet Jennings of *'Rectory Farm'*, born 13th Sep 1943.

20th August 1944 - Dennis Frederick Thompson
Son of Bert and Dorothy Thompson of North Brook End, born 12th Jul 1944.

27th August 1944 - Kenneth Dellar
Son of Rupert and Doris Dellar of *'Clifden Cottages'*, born 2nd Jul 1944.

10th September 1944 - Mary Elizabeth Venn
Daughter of Stanley and Phyllis Venn of *'Police Houses'*, Castle Hill, Cambridge, born 24th Apr 1944.

29th October 1944 - Kenneth Walter Woods
Son of Jim and Emily Woods of *'The Pear Tree'*, born 15th Sep 1944.

1st July 1945 - Gillian Merrill
Daughter of William and Eva Merrill of Brook End, born 17th May 1945.

29th July 1945 - Rita Colley
Daughter of Frank and Elsie Colley of Pound Green, born 2nd Jul 1945.

13th August 1945 - Frederick James Hunt
Son of Newton and Marjorie Hunt of *'Morden Hall'*, born 8th May 1945.

30th September 1945 - Evelyn Mary Covington
Daughter of Jack and Emily Covington of Church Street, born 25th Jul 1945.

12th May 1946 - Patricia Margaret White
Daughter of Joan White of *'Morden House'*, born 21st Nov 1942.

16th June 1946 - Colin William Chapman
Son of John and Olive Chapman of *'Avenel Place'*, born 28th Apr 1944.

1st September 1946 - Derek Watson
Son of Cliff and Kate Watson of *'The Red Barns'*, born 21st May 1946.

20th October 1946 - Susan Dianne Leonard
Daughter of Vic and Win Leonard of *'Phoenix Row'*, born 28th Jul 1946.

23rd January 1947 - Gloria Ann Thompson
Daughter of Sid and Lilian Thompson, born 22nd Jan 1947.

2nd February 1947 - John Frederick Kirbyshire
Son of Fred and Ellen Kirbyshire of *'The Brickyard'*, born 16th Dec 1946.

2nd March 1947 - George Noble
Son of Gordon and Mary Noble of High Street, born 19th Dec 1946.

16th March 1947 - Janet Patricia Thompson
Daughter of Bert and Dorothy Thompson of Nth Brook End, born 17th Dec 1946.

23rd Match 1947 - Lynda Averil Godman
Daughter of Neville and Brenda Godman of *'Cold Harbour'*, born 19th Dec 1946.

6th April 1947 - Michael Edward Sole
Son of Cecil and Betty Sole of Walsall (temporary), born 26th Dec 1946.

7th September 1947 - Mervyn Michael Leonard
Son of Tom and Mona Leonard of *'Fox Lea'*, born 17th July 1947.

20th September 1947 - Keith Howard Dellar
Son of Harry and Margaret Dellar of *'Robin Dell'*, born 28th Jul 1947.

28th March 1948 - Pamela Lilian Sole
Daughter of Cecil and Betty Sole of Litlington, born 1st Dec 1947.

16th May 1948 - Penelope Jane Hill
Daughter of Arthur and Susannah Hill of *'Fair View'*, born 28th Oct 1947.

17th June 1948 - Peter Herbert Kimross-Purser
Son of Peter and Doreen Kimross-Purser of *'Odsey House'*, born 11th Feb 1948.

8th August 1948 - Edward Keith Thompson
Son of Bert and Dorothy Thompson of North Brook End, born 31st May 1948.

7th November - Richard Kirbyshire
Son of Fred and Ellen Kirbyshire.

14th November 1948 - Trevor James Harrington
Son of Jack and Lilian Harrington.

27th February 1949 - Rita Kirbyshire
Daughter of Davis and Louise Kirbyshire of *'The Brickyard'*, born 23rd Dec 1948.

27th February 1949 - Philip Arthur Henman
Son of Arthur and Elsie Henman of New Road, born 14th Dec 1948.

3rd April 1949 - Michael Williams
Son of Edgar and Elizabeth Williams of Wendy Road, born 12th Feb 1949.

10th April 1949 - Frederick John Collings
Son of Fred and Elsie Collings of Letchworth, born 18th Sep 1937.

10th April 1949 - Michael John Dellar
Son of Cecil and Jean Dellar of Ashwell Road, born 7th Feb 1949.

22nd May 1949 - Winifred Norah Mynott
Daughter of Alf and Phyllis Mynott of Wendy Road, born 13th April 1949.

2nd October 1949 - Phyllis Norah Lilley
Daughter of Charley and Audrey Lilley of Silver Street, born 2nd Aug 1949.

11th December 1949 - Vera Joyce Hart
Daughter of Harry and Joyce Hart of Wendy Road, born 14th Jul 1949.

Weddings

We are indebted to the Royston Museum for providing access to their archives of the Royston Crow from which the following wedding reports were extracted.

14th February 1940 - Alec Jack Parrish and Floyd Hunt
'On Feb. 14th 1940, quietly, at St Marys Church, Guilden Morden, by the Rev Ll G S Price, MA., Alec Jack, third son of Mr and Mrs J Parrish, of Stanford Bury, Shefford, to Floyd, daughter of Mr and Mrs F W P Hunt, of North Brook End, Steeple Morden.'

13th July 1940 at Ashwell - Frank Henry Kirby and Edith May Davies
Frank was the son of Sidney and Bertha Kirby of Cold Harbour Farm. Edith was from Ashwell. Frank farmed at Morden Hall until he took over from his father at Cold Harbour. He was for many years a prominent member of the Parish Council. The picture shows them celebrating their Golden Wedding Anniversary.

3rd August 1940 - Albert Randall and Lizzie Frost

'At the Parish Church on Saturday morning, the wedding took place of Mr Albert Randall of Guilden Morden, and Miss Elisabeth Frost of Wimbish Green, Saffron Walden. The Rev. Ll G S Price performed the ceremony, and the bride was given away by Mr F Randall, brother of the bridegroom. As the wedding party left the church, a party of friends formed a guard of honour.'

21st September 1940 - Alfred William Mynott and Phyllis Maud Peckett

'A pretty wedding was solemnised at the Parish Church by the Rev. Ll G S Price (vicar), on Saturday. The contracting parties were A/c Alfred William Mynott, eldest son of Mr and Mrs J Mynott, of Shingay, and Miss Phyllis Maud Peckett, second daughter of Mr and Mrs J Peckett, of Council Houses, Wendy Road. The bride, who was given away by her father, wore a dress of white satin and lace net, and carried a bouquet of pink carnations. She was attended by her two sisters, the misses Dorothy Covington and Elsie Peckett, who wore dresses of blue marocain with silver headdress, and carried bouquets of asters. Best man was Mr Robin Mynott, brother of the bridegroom. On leaving the church, the bride was presented with a silver horseshoe by her little brother, John.'

28th Dec 1940 - John Christopher Harrington and Lilian Margaret Annie Sole

Jack was the son of Mr and Mrs James Harrington from Ireland. He left there in his mid teens, worked at Linden Hall Hotel in London as Head Porter, then for John Laing Builders, helping to build Steeple Morden Airfield. Lil was the eldest daughter of Mr and Mrs Alfred Sole. She worked at Morden House, then Letchworth Laundry. Jack served for many years on the Parish Council and the Village Hall Committee, where he was at various times Vice-Chairman, Chairman, Secretary and Treasurer, and Lil was the Caretaker.

1941 - Alexander Peter Fordham Watts and Prudence Mary MacDonald

Alexander was from Guilden Morden, Prudence from Sussex. The Marriage took place in Marylebone District, London.

8th February 1941 - James Harry Pelly Perrett and Freda Mary Manning

James was the son of Mr and Mrs James Perrett a Tobacconist from London. Fred was the daughter of Mr and Mrs Joseph Manning of High Street.

1st March 1941 - Sidney Jasper Worboys and Gladys Louisa Rosey Grocott
Sidney was the son of Mr and Mrs Frederick Worboys of Abington Pigotts. Glad was the daughter of Mr and Mrs Gordon Grocott.

7th June 1941 - Francis Edward Colley and Elsie Worboys
Frank and Elsie met when Frank was attached to a Searchlight Site at Shingay. He joined the Army in 1941 as a Gunner after working for LMS Railway in Stoke-on-Trent. Elsie served in the ATS having previously worked for Lewis Falk in Letchworth. She was the daughter of Mr and Mrs Alfred Worboys of Pound Green.

19th July 1941 - Sidney James Thompson and Lilian Gladys Bonfield
Sid was a Private in the Mobile Bath Unit. He was the son of Mr and Mrs Frank Thompson of Steeple Morden. Lilian was the daughter of Mr and Mrs Frank Bonfield of the *'Black Horse'* Public House. They are shown celebrating their Diamond Wedding Anniversary.

4th Sep 1941 in Ashford, Kent - Charles William Lilley and Iris Naomi Kemp

7th November 1941 - William James Gentle and Elsie Hilda Rayner
'The wedding was that of Mr. William James Gentle, of Orchard House, Guilden Morden, and Miss Elsie Rayner, of 'Killarney', Guilden Morden. Both the bridegroom and the bride are natives of the village, and from their earliest days, in one sphere and another, have been actively associated with the village life and the Congregational Church, in particular. Mr. Gentle is the fourth son of the late Mr. and Mrs. Jas. Gentle, the former having been a well-known and respected deacon of the church. The bridegroom is the superintendent of the Congregational Sunday School, a post he has filled for many years; secretary of Guilden Morden branch of the British Legion, and treasurer of the Village Hall committee. In other ways also he has assisted in the welfare of the village. The bride is the youngest daughter of the late Mr. and Mrs. Fredk. Rayner, of Guilden Morden, and was formerly a Sunday School teacher. Mr. Rayner was a well-known local farmer, and he and Mrs. Rayner were connected with the Guilden Morden Congregational Church. The bride has also taken an interest in local affairs, especially those connected with the Congregational Church.'

24th November 1941 - Arthur Claude Pearce and Kathleen Florence Millns
Claude was a CSM in the RASC the son of Arthur Pearce of Trap Road. Kathleen, known as 'Bink', was a widow,

the daughter of Mr and Mrs Ernest Healey, who was a garage proprietor of Trap Road. The picture shows them celebrating twenty one years at the *'Three Tuns'*.

29th November 1941 - Herbert Frank Thompson and Dorothy May Peckett

Herbert was a horsekeeper for Mr Hunt at North Brook End Farm. He was from the *'Pear Tree'* Public House, the son of Mr and Mrs Frank Thompson, who was also a horsekeeper. Dorothy was also from the *'Pear Tree'*, the daughter of Mr and Mrs Joseph Peckett. She was in service at the Hunt's North Brook End Farm.

1942 - Brian Worboys and Helen Eva Revels

Brian was from Ashwell Road, Guilden Morden and Helen was from Ashwell.

March 1942 - Sidney Gentle and Eileen Alma Booker

Sidney was a Guilden Morden man and Eileen came from Ashwell where the wedding took place.

1942 at Ashwell - Thomas Leonard and Mona Marjorie May Mitchell

Tom was the son of Edith Leonard of Guilden Morden. He worked for the Letchworth firm of Bennett's and was the leader of the church bellringers. Mona was the daughter of Percy and Ruby Mitchell from Ashwell. They set up home at *'Foxlea'*.

14th March 1942 - Walter William Southgate and Mary Ann Croshaw

Walter was a gardener and the son of the late Walter Southgate, a brewer. Mary was a widow from Phoenix Terrace, the daughter of the late Richard Hart, a collier.

25th April 1942 - Ernest Henry Dore and Elizabeth Ruth Merrill

'The Parish Church had been tastefully decorated with spring floweres for the wedding, which took place on Saturday, of Private Ernest Henry Dore of the Herts. and Beds. Regiment, son of Mr. Ernest Henry Dore and the late Mrs. Dore, of Kentish Town, London, and Miss Elizabeth Ruth Merrill, youngest daughter of Mr. and Mrs. R.B. Merrill, of Wendy Road, Guilden Morden. The ceremony was performed by the Rev. Ll G S Price. The bride, who was given away by her father. Mr. Percy Hayden, cousin of the bridgroom, was best man. As the couple left the church they were presented with a silver horseshoe by Miss Margaret Ann Merrill, the niece of the bride.'

13th May 1942 - Gunner Stanley Worboys and Edna Mary Watts
'The Congregational Church was the scene of a pretty wedding on Tuesday, when the contracting parties were Gunner Stanley Worboys, son of the late Mr. F.E. Worboys, of High Street, and Miss Edna Mary Watts, daughter of Mr. and Mrs. F. Watts, also of High Street. The ceremony was performed by the Rev. H.F. Hawkes, Mr. O. Kaye being at the organ. The bride, who was given away by her father, wore a dress of powder-blue with hat to match, and carried a bouquet of pink carnations. Miss Joan Watts, sister of the bride, wore a soft shade of brick with hat to match, and carried a bouquet of apricot carnations. Mr. A.W. Conder, a friend of the bridegroom, was best man.'

12th September 1942 - Charles Harold Pettengell and Emma Violet Izzard
Charlie (37) was the son of Mr and Mrs George Pettengell of Church Lane. Emma (44) was the daughter of Mr and Mrs William Izzard of Church Street.

25th Dec 1942 at Arrington - Douglas William Bonfield and Irene Mary Charter
Doug was the son of Frederick and Edith Bonfield of *'Phoenix Row'*, Guilden Morden. Rene was the daughter of Augustus and Susan Charter of Arrington.

27th Feb 1943 - Private Neville John Godman and Brenda Rigby Darby
'A colourful wedding took place at the Parish Church, on Saturday last, when the contracting parties were Private Neville John Godman only son of Mr. and Mrs. John Godman, Silver Street, and Miss Brenda Rigby Darby, daughter of Mr. and Mrs. W. Webb, Cold Harbour. The officiating clergyman was the Rev. Ll G S Price. There were four bridesmaids, Barbara Covington, niece of the bridegroom, Mavis Warden, niece of the bride, Mrs. Tom Leonard and Miss Daphne Mitchell. The best man was Mr. Tom Leonard.'

17th April 1943 - Frederick Newton Hunt and Marjorie Lilian Kirby
Newton, as he was known, was the son of Frederick and Sally Hunt of North Brook End Farm, Steeple Morden. He took over the farm from his father. Marjorie was the daughter of Sid and Bertha Kirby of Cold Harbour Farm. She was a nurse in the Red Cross during the Second World War. They eventually set up home in a bungalow in Wendy Road (now New Road).

26th June 1943 - Maurice Fred Dennis and Phyllis Vera May Huffer
'A very pretty wedding, by special licence, was solemnized at the Congregational Church on Saturday last, June 26th, by the Rev. H.F. Hawkes. The contracting parties were Private Maurice Fred Dennis, Beds, and Herts. Regiment,

only son of Mr. and Mrs. F. Dennis of Valley Farm, and Miss Phyllis May Huffer, only daughter of Mr. and Mrs. A. Huffer, of Pound Green. She was attended by her niece, Miss Marie Huffer. The duties of best man were carried out by Mr. Robert Williams, friend of the bridegroom.'

19th October 1944 - William Arthur Dellar and Maud Thompson

Arthur (43) was the eldest son of William and Florence Dellar of Ashwell Road. Maud (44) was the daughter Mr and Mrs David Thompson.

31st March 1945 - Frederick Leslie Kirbyshire and Ellen Mary Starr

'A pretty wedding took place at St. Mary's Church on Saturday, March 31st., the bride being Ellen Mary, eldest daughter of Mr. and Mrs. Arthur Law, of 'Dove Cottage,' Guilden Morden, and the bridegroom, Frederick Leslie, fourth son of Mr. and the late Mrs. Arthur Kirbyshire, of the 'Brickfields,' Guilden Morden. The bride was attended by her sister, Miss Joyce Law, and her cousin, Miss Betty Peckett.'

26th May 1945 at Bassingbourn - Horace George Matthews and Winifred May Christine Racher

Horace was the son of the late William and Agnes Matthews from Church Street. Winnie was the daughter of Bertie and Beatrice Racher from Kneesworth.

1945 - Edgar Charles Albon Barratt and Gwendoline Edith Hebditch

Edgar was the son of Allan and Ruth Barratt and Gwen was from London.

25th September 1945 - William Frederick Connor and Isabel Alice Clarke

William (65) was a widower and farmer of *'Town Farm'*. His father William was also a farmer. Isabel (53) was the housekeeper at *'Town Farm'*.

1946 - Sgt Hal Franklyn Lurmon and Vera Winifred Lindsay

Frank was the son of Mr and Mrs Harvey Franklyn Lurmon of Dallas, Texas. Vera was the only daughter of Mr and Mrs George Lindsay. They were married at Guilden Morden Congregational Church.

18th May 1946 - Cecil Charles Edward Sole and Betty Cosford

Cecil was the son of Mr and Mrs Alf Sole of Ashwell Road. He had been a Japanese prisoner of war. Betty worked at Morden House.

6th July 1946 - Jack Newell and Lily Christine Worboys

Jack was the son of Mr and Mrs Alfred Newell of Steeple Morden. He was a stockman. Christine, as she was known, was the daughter of Mr and Mrs Albert Worboys of Ashwell Road.

August 1947 - Albert Kirbyshire and Evelyn Grace Sadler

Alf was the son of Mr and Mrs Arthur Kirbyshire of Guilden Morden. He was a driver in the RASC during the Second World War. Evelyn was from Holt in Norfolk where the wedding was held.

20th Aug 1947 - Frederick Lawrence Chamberlain and Daphne Kaye

Fred was a draughtsman, the son of Mr and Mrs David Chamberlain of Letchworth. Daphne was the daughter Mr and Mrs Oswald Kaye the village blacksmith. She served for many years on the Parish Council, many of them as the Village Hall Committee representative on the Parish Council.

1948 - Charles William Lilley and Audrey May Thompson in Cambridge

Charlie was the son of James and Naomi Lilley of Silver Street. He was a Driver in the RASC during the Second World War. Audrey was the daughter of Frank and Ada Thompson.

10th July 1948 - Stanley Watts and Irene Hilda Harding

Stan was the son of Mr and Mrs Fred Watts of High Street. He served in the Army in the Second World War. Rene was the daughter of Mr and Mrs James Harding.

31st July 1948 - Arthur Henman and Elsie Priscilla Peckett

Arthur was the son of Mr and Mrs William Henman of Wrestlingworth. Elsie was the daughter of Mr and Mrs Joseph Peckett.

18th Dec 1948 - Harry William Arthur Butt and Winifred Ruby May Horsley
Harry was the son of Mr and Mrs Harry Butt of Clothall. Winifred was a Baker's Assistant, the daughter of Mr and Mrs Henry Horsley.

1949 - Montagu George Crittall and Doreen Frances Letts
Monty was the tenant at *'Rectory Farm'* and was a member of the Parish Council. Doreen was from Leicester.

2nd April 1949 - Thomas Anthony Carr and Nora Audrey Mary Tomlin
Thomas was a member of the American Air Force based at Steeple Morden. Nora was a machinist from *'Duck Lake Farm'*, daughter of Mr and Mrs Reg Tomlin.

1949 - Frederick James Bonfield and Kathleen Ada Warren
Fred was the son of Frederick and Edith Bonfield of *'Phoenix Row'*, (Frederick senior was killed in the First World War). Kath came from Wrestlingworth where the wedding took place.

18th June 1949 - Joseph George Pratt and Kathleen Mary Saville
Joseph was from Arrington, the son of Mr and Mrs Charles Pratt. Kathleen was a Land Worker from *'Robin Dell'*, the daughter of Mr and Mrs Edward Saville.

1st October 1949 - Walter Covington and Joyce Lillian Law
Walter was a steel worker from Scunthorpe, the son of Mr and Mrs Arthur Covington. Joyce was the daughter of Mr and Mrs Arthur Law of *'Dove Cottage'*, Guilden Morden.

Deaths

We are indebted to the Royston Museum for providing access to their archives of the Royston Crow from which the following obituaries were extracted.

27th January 1940 - Mrs Ethel Price at the *'Vicarage'*

'We record with deep regret, as the result of an accident, the death on Saturday last, of Ethel, wife of the Rev. Ll G S Price, vicar of Guilden Morden. Mrs Price was descending the stairs in her home in the evening of last Tuesday week when she missed the last step,

and fell. She was immediately assisted into the living-room, and the doctor was sent for. He diagnosed breakage of the right hip-bone, and advised her immediate removal to hospital. An ambulance was phoned for, and she was taken to a private ward in Addenbrookes, where the breakage was confirmed by X-ray and the limb set. Being very frail at the time, she became semi-conscious, and remained so until she passed away.

Born in Ipswich in 1864, daughter of C H Cowill, Esq., J.P. and several times Mayor of the town, niece of Professor Cowill, of Calcutta and Cambridge Universities, the great Orientalist, she seemed to combine in herself the sterling Christian character of her mother, and the high intellectual abilities of her father. Educated at the Ipswich High School and Cheltenham College, she graduated at the University of London. She took up the profession of a teacher, and was employed in the Durham High School, and also at Leicester, where she received the call to be a missionary, and offered to the Church Missionary Society, who sent her out to the Sarah Tucker at Palaincottah, South India. The missionaries of that place hearing that one called a 'new woman' and a 'blue stocking' was coming into their midst, were somewhat perturbed and alarmed, and with wondering thoughts went to meet her at the station. On her arrival, they were introduced to a beautiful lady with bright complexion and chestnut hair, and were suitably impressed. On further acquaintance, they found her quite different from what they has expected, and learnt to admire her humble spirit, her earnest devotion, and high intellectual abilities, being delighted with her singing, for she was gifted with a lovely voice, sweet and clear as a bell. After a few years, she married Mr Price, a missionary there. It had been proposed that she should not learn Tamil, the language spoken in South India, but concentrate her efforts on teaching the Indian girls the English language. To this she demurred, as she realised how impossible it would be to get at the hearts of the people unless she could speak to them in their own tongue. After marriage, she set herself to work amongst the women, who were charmed with her beautiful and scholarly Tamil. One often wondered how intimate was her knowledge of all their children, asking after each one by name. The secret of this, never divulged by her, was the fact that she prayed for them, each one regularly by turn. She is still remembered affectionately by the women out there who greatly sorrowed when, after 25 years of service, she left with her husband for England, owing to the necessity of providing a home for her children. In October 1919, she came to Guilden Morden, and did her utmost in helping her husband in his work. She took a keen interest in the Mothers' Union, and did much to foster its work in Guilden Morden. She will be missed in the village, and many will arise and call her blessed. She leaves her husband, a daughter and 3 sons, to whom we extend our deepest sympathy. The funeral will take place at the Parish Church, Guilden Morden, today at 3pm.

The inquest was held on Wednesday morning at Addenbrookes Hospital, when Dr W H Bower said that the deceased was admitted to a private ward at Addenbrookes Hospital on Jan 23rd. She was rather shocked and had a fractured right femur. She died on Saturday last, the cause of death being shock due to the fracture. Recording a verdict of 'Accidental Death,' the Coroner extended his sympathy to the Rev. Price.'

'Amid many manifestations of sympathy and respect, the funeral took place at Guilden Morden Parish Church on Friday afternoon, of Ethel Price, wife of the Rev. Ll G S Price, vicar of Guilden Morden. Her death, as the result of an accident, was recorded in our last

issue. The service was conducted by the Rev. J E Cowell, of Cotton Rectory, Stowmarket, (brother of Mrs Price) and assisted by Bishop H McG E Price, Assistant Bishop of Ely. Mr O Kaye was the organist. Bishop Price referred to the deceased's long and faithful service of the Lord, saying that she had been a splendid partner to her husband, both in India and this country, her only object being the promotion of the Kingdom. The immediate mourners were: The Rev. Ll G S Price, (widower), Miss Dorothea Price, (daughter), Mr Christopher Price, Mr and Mrs Edward Price, and Mr Davis Price, (sons and daughter-in-law). Half muffled peals in memoriam were rung on Sunday morning at the Parish Church at the request of the bell-ringers.'

5th February 1940 - Mrs Elizabeth Clark at '8 Avenel Terrace'
'We record with regret the death of Mrs F J Clark, which took place at her home on Monday last week at the age of 70. Deceased, who was a native of the village, had been a great sufferer in recent years, but her final illness was of short duration. She leaves a husband and one son, for whom the greatest sympathy is felt. The funeral service at the Congregational Church, was conducted by Rev. F Cranham of Litlington. The principal mourners were Mr F J Clark (husband), Mr H Clark (son), Mr and Mrs M Clark (brother-in-law and sister-in-law), Messrs S R and C Clark (nephews), Mrs S Clark (niece).'

25th February 1940 - Mrs Ellen Thompson at '6 Council Houses'
'We record the death of Mrs D Thompson, of 6 Council Cottages, Ashwell Road, which took place on Sunday February 25th, at the age of 75. Deceased had not enjoyed good health for some considerable time, but her final illness was not of long duration, and ended in a peaceful passing. The funeral service at the parish church Thursday last week was conducted by the vicar, the Rev Ll G S Price. The principal mourners were: Mr Davis Thompson snr, (husband), Messrs Edward, Frank and David Thompson (sons), Misses Sarah, Alice and Maud Thompson (daughters), Mrs E Thompson and Mrs F Thompson (daughters-in-law), Mr H Thompson (grandson), Mr W Thompson (nephew), Mesdames Peel, Saville, Moule and Chapman (nieces).'

5th March 1940 - Miss Aphia Whyte Fisk at 'Morden House'

6th March 1940 - Frank Hayward at the 'Six Bells'

7th March 1940 - Martha Ellen Pettengell Morris of High Street
'By the death of Mrs W Morris of High Street, Guilden Morden, which occurred at her home on Thursday in last week, the village has lost a well-known and beloved resident. Mrs Morris was 80 years of age, and had lived in the village practically the whole of her life. Despite her age she was most active and was about doing her household duties on the Sunday before her death. The same day she attended worship at the Congregational Chapel, of which she was a regular attendant and member, and her death came as a great shock to the village. She leaves two sons and five daughters. Amid many manifestations of respect, the funeral took place on Monday, the service in the chapel prior to the interment being

conducted by the Rev. F Cranham (Litlington), assisted by the Rev. Ll G S Price. The family mourners were Messrs Herbert and Frank Morris (sons), Mrs Penn, Mrs Dinnage, Mrs Bullock, Mrs Mence (daughters), Mrs H Morris (daughter-in-law), Mr and Mrs L Izzard (brother and sister-in-law), Mr B Clark, Mr and Mrs F Clark (nephews and niece), Mr E Desborough (cousin), Mrs J Levy, the Misses A and E Levy, Mr W Levy, Miss King, Miss I Pateman, Mrs A Cole (friends). Miss Millie Morris (daughter) was unable to attend.'

8th March 1940 - Charlotte Hannah Hadley at *'Morden House'*

14th March 1940 - George James Lee at Pound Green, gardener
'We record the passing of Mr G J Lee, of Pound Green, whose death took place at his home on Thursday of last week, at the age of 73 years. The interment took place in the cemetery, the service being conducted by the Rev. F Cranham of Litlington. The principal mourners were: the widow, Messrs F and C Lee (sons), Mrs Chapman, Mrs Monk and Mrs Green (daughters), Mrs C Lee (daughter-in-law), Mr A Jarman, Mrs W Carter, Mrs S Carter, Miss C Carter.'

5th April 1940 - Mrs Maria Theresa Collins at *'Morden House'*

19th May 1940 - Mrs Sarah Jane Starr of Flex Lane, Steeple Morden, at Meldreth
'The passing of Mrs Sarah Jane Starr, widow of the late Mr F Starr, of Flex Lane, Steeple Morden, severs another link with the past. The deceased, who, since the death of her husband some 12 years ago, had lived with her daughter, Mrs W Marsh, High Street, Meldreth, where she died after a short illness on May 19th, at the age of 85. The interment took place at Guilden Morden, last Friday, the funeral service being conducted by the Rev. Ll G S Price. The principal mourners were Mr and Mrs S Starr (son and daughter-in-law), Mr and Mrs J Oyston, Mr and Mrs W Marsh, Mr and Mrs A Clements (daughters and sons-in-law), Mrs W Hunt and Mr C Noble.'

28th May 1940 - Jessie Bright Fairbank at *'Morden House'*

4th July 1940 - George William Covington at Ashwell Road
'The death took place of Mr G Covington of Ashwell Road, at his home on Thursday last, at the age of 70 years. Although he had not enjoyed good health for some time, he had carried on his work and his sudden passing was a shock. Sympathy is felt for his widow and family of two sons and four daughters. The interment took place at the cemetery on Monday, preceded by a service at the house conducted by Rev. H F Hawkes, the new Congregational minister. The principal mourners were: Mrs G Covington (widow), Messrs Arthur and Herbert Covington (sons), Mrs G Andrews, Mrs K Askew, Mrs G King, Miss I Covington (daughters), Messrs W and A Covington (brothers), Mrs A Bonnet, Mrs F Starr, Mrs G Bird (sisters), Miss D and Mr K Andrews (grand-children), Mr K Askew (son-in-law), Messrs D & E Saville (brothers-in-law), Mrs A Covington, Mrs H Covington (daughters-

in-law), Mrs K Chapman, Mrs F Huckle, Mrs E Saville (sisters-in-law), Mrs W Conder, Mrs G Watson, Mrs W Chapman, Mrs R Bedford, Mrs A Law (nieces), Mr W Chapman (nephew), Mr C Watts and Mr E Pepper.'

25th July 1940 - George Pettengell

'The death took place of Mr G Pettengell, of Guilden Morden, at his home on Thursday, at the age of 77 years. Mr Pettengell was at one time gardener for Mr W A Sandeman, at Morden House. He had been in ill health for a long time. He leaves a widow, three sons, and three daughters, for whom much sympathy is felt. The funeral service at the Parish Church on Tuesday was conducted by the Rev Ll G S Price. The principal mourners were: Mrs Pettengell (widow), Messrs. A C and P Pettengell (sons), Misses M and E Pettengell, Mrs Westerman (daughters), Mrs Sadler (sister), Mr F Sole (brother-in-law), Mrs A Pettengell, Mrs P Pettengell (daughters-in-law), Mr E Westerman (son-in-law), Miss Pat Pettengell, Miss Joyce and Master E Westerman (grand-children), Mrs W Whitbread, Mrs J Pratt (sisters-in-law), and Miss Izzard (a friend).'

10th August 1940 - Frederick Rayner

'The funeral took place at Guilden Morden on Wednesday last week of Mr Fred Rayner of Great Green, Guilden Morden, who passed away at the age of 79 years. By the passing of Mr Fred Rayner, the village has lost another old and respected inhabitant. Since his boyhood days which were spent at Shingay where he was born, he had seen many changes. He had worked with the fossil diggers, and as a young man had made a trip to America in company with his brother, the late Mr John Rayner, and others of a like spirit. Those were times when such a voyage was a real adventure. Returning to this country, he settled down, and by dint of patience and perseverance, achieved a measure of success as a smallholder and farmer. In his dealings with his fellows, he was known for his uprightness and integrity, and was held in high esteem. His failing strength had been evident for some months, and he passed away at his home on Saturday, Aug. 10th.

The Service - The funeral service at the Congregational Church, of which the deceased was a member, was conducted by the Rev. H F Hawkes, a short address being given by the vicar, the Rev, Ll G S Price. The immediate mourners were: Mr H Rayner (son), Mrs E Robinson, Mrs G Barnes and Miss E H Rayner (daughters), Mr H Robinson (grandson), Mrs A Haylock (sister), Mrs J Gentle snr., (sister-in-law), Mr A Haylock, Mr J Gentle snr., (brothers-in-law), Messrs F Rayner, W J Thompson, J Gentle jnr., (nephews), Mrs S Clark (niece), Mr G Barnes (son-in-law), Mrs J Gentle jnr., (niece)....'

10th September 1940 - Eleanor Cardine Paget (nun) at 'Morden House'

18th September 1940 - Mrs Amelia Wedge at New Road

'The death took place on Wednesday last week, following an illness cheerfully and patiently borne, of Mrs T Wedge of New Road, Guilden Morden, at the age of 76 years. Mrs Wedge had been in failing health for some time. In earlier years she had been an active worker in the Salvation Army, and since residing in the village had been a member of the Women's

Guild of the Congregational Church. Her cheerful personality will be greatly missed by all who knew her. The funeral service on Saturday was conducted at the house by Captain Smithwick, assisted by the vicar, the Rev. Ll G S Price, and the Rev. H F Hawkes (Congregational Minister). The band of the Potton Corps accompanied the singing and preceded the cortege to the cemetery. The principal mourners were: Mr T Wedge (husband), Mr and Mrs T Wedge jun. (son and daughter-in-law), Mr and Mrs G Wedge jun. (son and daughter-in-law), Mrs W Pearce (daughter), Mr S Watts (grandson). Miss G Wedge (grand-daughter), Mrs A Pearce, Mrs Pepperell and Mrs E Harris.'

14th October 1940 - Alice Amelia Taylor at *'Morden House'*

6th November 1940 - Mrs Alice Esther Simpson at *'Morden House'*

21st January 1941 - Herbert George Clark at *'Avenel Terrace'*
'The funeral took place on Saturday, of Mr. H.G. Clark, only son of Mr. F. Clark, of 8 Avenel Terrace, and the late Mrs. Clark, who passed away after a short illness, at his home, at the age of 44 years, on Tuesday last week. Herbert, as he was known to all, was a favourite in the village, and in spite of his physical disabilities, maintained a steady cheerfulness and patient perseverance, worthy of admiration. His gifts of memorising and elocution had often given pleasure to many, and his last appearance at a Fellowship meeting at the Congregational Church will be remembered by those who heard him. The funeral service was conducted by the Rev. H.F. Hawkes. The principal mourners were Mr. F. Clark (father), Mr. and Mrs. M. Clark (uncle and aunt), Mr. and Mrs. R. Clark, Messrs. S. Clark, C. Clark and F. Clark (cousins), Mr. and Mrs. Forrest and Miss Izzard.'

1st March 1941 - William Charles Stockwell, at Addenbrooke's Hospital
'The funeral took place at the Parish Church on Friday, of Mr. W.C. Stockwell, of Little Green, who died at Addenbrooke's Hospital on the previous Saturday, at the age of 59. Mr. Stockwell was a native of Winchester, Hants. and was well-known in Royston and district. The Rev. Ll.G.S. Price conducted the service, Miss Price presiding at the organ. The principal mourners were Mrs. Stockwell (widow), Mr. S. Stockwell (son), Mrs. S. Leonard (daughter), Mrs. S. Stockwell (daughter-in-law), Mr. S. Leonard (son-in-law), Mr. F. Stockwell (brother), Mrs. F. Stockwell, Mrs G. Head (sisters-in-law), Master Teddy Stockwell (nephew), Mr. G. Endersby and Mrs. H. Brim, of Wrestlingworth.'

10th March 1941 - Miss Annie Louise Pool at *'Morden House'*

21st March 1941 - Miss Fanny Elizabeth Worboys

27th March 1941 - Mrs Mary Elizabeth Ingram at *'Morden House'*

10th April 1941 - Ephraim Skinner at High Street

'The death occurred on Thursday last week, of Mr. Ephraim Skinner, of High Street, at the age of 87 years. Mr. Skinner was a native of Abington Pigotts, and had resided in the village since his retirement from the railway, where he was a guard. He was of a kindly disposition, and although failing in health had lately confined him to his home, he will be missed by all who knew him. The funeral at the Parish Church was conducted by the Rev. Ll.G.S. Price. Miss Price was at the organ. Messrs. Albert, Frederick and Arthur Skinner (sons), Mrs. H. Roberts (daughter), Mrs. F. Skinner (daughter-in-law), Mr. H. Roberts (son-in-law), Mr. G. Moule (nephew) and Mrs. Beales.'

8th July 1941 - Thomas Wedge of New Road, at Cambridge, stone worker

'The funeral took place on Saturday of the late Mr T Wedge of New-road, who passed away at Cambridge on Tuesday week at the age of 77 years. Since the death of Mrs Wedge, he had had indifferent health. The service on Saturday was conducted by the Captain of the Potton Corps of the Salvation Army, assisted by the vicar the Rev. Ll G S Price and the Congregational Minister, the Rev. H F Hawkes. The Salvation Army band accompanied the singing, and also preceded the cortege to the cemetery. The principal mourners were: Mr W T Wedge and Mrs W Pearce (son and daughter), Mr and Mrs G Wedge (son and daughter-in-law), Mr and Mrs Walls, Mr F Pearce (grand-children)....'

13th July 1941 - Thomas Wright at Church Terrace, wheelwright

'In the passing of Mr. T. Wright of Church Street, whose death occurred at his home on Sunday week, at the age of 74 years, the village has lost another outstanding personality. Mr. Wright had held office as churchwarden for many years and was also a member of the Parish Council. In both of these offices, he held the respect of his fellow members through his loyalty and devotion. The funeral service at the Parish Church on Thursday last, was conducted by the Rev, Ll.G.S. Price. Miss Price presided at the organ. The principal mourners were: Mrs. T. Wright (widow), Mr. and Mrs. A.T. Wright (son and daughter-in-law), Miss Joan and Mr Aubrey Wright (grandchildren), Mr. and Mrs. Peel (uncle and aunt), Mrs. Allen and Mrs. Merrill.'

31st July 1941 - Mrs Selina Winders at Guilden Morden

'The village of Guilden Morden has lost another highly respected member, by the passing of Mrs. J. Winders, whose death occurred at her home, on Thursday last week, at the age of 78. She had been in failing health for some time, and her suffering was patiently borne. The second daughter of the late Mr. and Mrs. Stonebridge, of Biggleswade, Mrs. Winders had resided in the village some 56 years, and for most of this period had been a member and loyal supporter of the Congregational Church, having formerly been a member of the Biggleswade Old Meeting. The funeral service at the Congregational Church on Monday, was conducted by the Rev. H.F. Hawkes. In his address, he paid tribute to the sincere Christian character of Mrs. Winders, and spoke of the loss the church had sustained. The Principal mourners were: Mrs. F.C. Larkinson and Mrs A.D. Horton (sisters), Mr. F.W. Endersby, Mr. A, D. Horton, Mr. W. Flint (brothers-in-law), Messrs. E.F. Endersby, S.D.

Horton, A.D. Denny, W.G. Cartwright (nephews), Miss C. Larkinson, Mrs. A.C. Denny, Mrs. H. Larkinson, Mrs. E. Rhodes (nieces), Mr. J.B. Larkinson, Mr, and Mrs. J.S. Larkinson, Miss A.Larkinson, Mr. C. Larkinson, Mr. W. Carter, Mr. and Mrs. W. Pettengell, Mr. and Mrs. G.J. Pooley, Mr. J. Gentle, Mr, Hart, Mrs. Croshaw and Miss S. Holder. Mr. J. Winders (widower) was unable to attend on account of ill-health.'

17th Aug 1941 - Mrs Bertha Day at the Post Office, wife of Harry Pilch Day

31st December 1941 - Alfred Thompson at Peckham

'The funeral took place at the Congregational Church on Tuesday, of Mr. A. Thompson, a former resident of the village, whose death occurred at his home in London on December 31st at the age of 51 years. Mr. Thompson had been gradually failing for some time, but had continued working up to December 26th, and the end came rather suddenly. He leaves a widow, four sons and three daughters, for whom much sympathy is felt. He was a native of Guilden Morden, being the youngest son of the late Mr. and Mrs Isaac Thompson, and his wife was the eldest daughter of the late Mr. W. Matthews and of Mrs. Matthews, of Church Street. For the past 26 years, he has been in the employ of the Southern Railway Company, on police duty, and earned the respect and esteem of all who knew him. The funeral was conducted by the Rev. H.F. Hawkes. The mourners were: Mrs. A. Thompson (widow), Mr. Arthur, Cyril and Dennis Thompson (sons), Miss Joan Thompson (daughter), Mrs. Dowdy, Mrs. Manning (sisters), Mr. E. Thompson (brother), Mr. J. Matthews, C.S.M. V. Matthews, Mr. H. Matthews and Mr. Hawkins (brother-in-law), Mesdames J. Matthews, V. Matthews, Hawkins, Bowen and W. Saunders (sisters-in-law), Mr. P. Ilett (brother-in-law), Mr. H. Ilett (nephew), Mr. and Mrs. F. Izzard, Miss M. Izzard (niece), Miss Elsie Manning, Mrs. Perritt, Mrs. D. Thompson (cousins), Mr. W. Thompson, senior, and Mr. E. Matthews (uncles).'

30th January 1942 - Mrs Rose Emily Rogers at High Street

7th March 1942 - Simeon George Dellar, butcher

'The remains of Mr. Simeon George Dellar, of High Street, who died at the age of 74 years, were laid to rest in the churchyard on Wednesday last week. The service was conducted by the Rev. Ll.G.S. Price. The family mourners were: Mrs. S.G. Dellar (widow), Mr, and Mrs. W.G. Dellar (son and daughter-in-law), Mr. and Mrs. F. Watts and Mr. and Mrs. C. Izzard (sons-in-law and daughters), Mrs. H. Whitworth (daughter), Messrs. C. and S. Watts (grandsons), Misses J. Watts and J. Dellar (grand-daughters), Mr. A. Leonard (brother-in-law), and Mr. and Mrs. F. Webb (nephew and niece).'

8th April 1942 - Mrs Mary Ann Southgate at 'Windy Ridge'

'Sympathy is extended to Mr. W. Southgate, at the loss of his wife, less than a month after the anniversary of their wedding day. The death occurred at their home on Wednesday last week, at the age of 61 years. The funeral service was conducted by the vicar the Rev. Ll.G.S. Price , Miss Price presiding at the organ. The principal mourners were: Mr. W. Southgate

(widower), Mr. S. and Mr. H. Croshaw (sons), Mrs. Bradford (daughter), Mr. P. and Mr. and Mrs. H. Hart (brothers and sister-in-law), Mrs. S. and Mrs. H. Croshaw (daughter-in-law), Mrs. P. Southgate aand Mrs. P. Croshaw (granddaughters), Mr. A. and Mr. C. Southgate (stepsons), Mr. and Mrs. G. Hart (nephew and niece), Mr. and Mrs. V. Leonard, Mr. and Mrs. H. Bonfield and Mr. H. Dellar.'

12th April 1942 - Mrs Evelyn Foggin at *'Morden House'*

15th April 1942 - Geoffrey Edward Rayner at Ashwell Road
'A statement that his son was worried because he had been classed as Grade II, and not AI, for the army, was made by a father at an inquest on Geoffrey Edward Rayner, aged 19, of Council Houses, Guilden Morden, and the Coroner, Mr Jasper Lyon, returned a verdict of 'Suicide while the balance of his mind was disturbed.' It was stated that Rayner, who was a draughtsman, was found shot dead at his home on Wednesday morning last week, with a service rifle between his legs. A piece of string connected the trigger to his left foot. Frank Rayner, father of the young man, of the same address, said that on Tuesday night his son complained of pains in the back. He had previously consulted a doctor for stomach pain. He had been passed Grade II for the army, and had been worried because he was not AI. Witness did not hear anything unusual during the night, but when he came down in the morning he found his son dead in an armchair. He was a member of the Home Guard.

The funeral took place on Saturday, the first part of the service being held at the Congregational Church, the Rev. G S Hawkes, assisted by the Rev. Ll G S Price, conducted. Mr O Kaye was the organist. A contingent of the Home Guard, under Captain Jennings, attended. The chief mourners were, Mr and Mrs F Rayner (father and mother), Mr and Mrs S Lindsay (brother-in-law and sister), Bramwell Harvey and Pearl Harvey (friends), Mr and Mrs A Cole (grandparents), Mr and Mrs R Peck, Mrs Sibley, Mr and Mrs G Reynolds, Mr and Mrs H Gentle, Mr and Mrs A Covington, Mr and Mrs W Cole (uncles and aunts), Master B Reynolds and J Cole (cousins)....'

18th April 1942 - Mabel Anna Brown at *'Morden House'*

12th May 1942 - Mrs Agnes Watts at 81a Mill Road, Cambridge
'The funeral took place at the Congregational Church on Saturday of Mrs. E. Watts, who died at Addenbrooke's Hospital, Cambridge, on the previous Tuesday, at the age of 63 years. The service was conducted by the Rev. H.F. Hawkes. Mr. O. Kaye presiding at the organ. The chief mourners were Mr. E. Watts (widower), Mr. A. Watts (son), Mrs. A. Evans and Mrs F. Chappell (daughters), Mr. A. Izzard (brother), Mr. G. Watts (father-in-law), Mr. and Mrs. T. Hyde, Mr. and Mrs. F. Watts, Mr. H. Watts, Miss F. Watts, Mr. and Mrs. L. Leete, Mrs. S. Stockwell, Mrs. G. Izzard (brothers and sisters-in-law).'

8th June 1942 - John William Lilley of Silver Street, labourer and chimney sweep
'The funeral took place at the Parish Churchyard on Friday, of Mr. J. W. Lilley, of Silver Street, who passed away at Addenbrooke's Hospital on the previous Monda y at the age of

68 years. The service was conducted by the Rev. Ll.G.S. Price, vicar. The mourners were Mrs. Lilley (widow), Messrs. Gordon, Charles and Cecil Lilley (sons), Mrs. W.G. Watts and Mrs. H. Hart (daughters), Mrs. R. Gwynn and Mrs Kember (sisters), Mrs. C. Lilley (daughter-in-law), Mr. M. Kember (nephew), and Mrs. L. Tuck and Miss Gwynn (nieces).'

29th June 1942 - Albert George Starr of *'Swan Fields'*, labourer and horsekeeper

'The sudden passing of Mr. A. Starr of 'Swan Fields' on Monday June 29th cast a gloom over the whole village. Deceased, who was well known and highly respected, had appeared to be in his usual health, although he had turned 70, and still carried on in his employment as horsekeeper at Town Farm. He collapsed near his home on Monday evening, and when assistance was summoned life was found to be extinct. A post mortem examination revealed the cause of death to be a ruptured heart. He leaves a widow, one son, and two daughters, for whom the greatest sympathy is felt. The funeral service at the Congregational Church on Friday was conducted by the Rev. H.F. Hawkes. Mr. O. Kaye presided at the organ. The principal mourners were Mrs. A. Starr (widow), Mr. S. Starr (son), Mrs. A. Baulk and Miss D. Starr (daughters), Mrs. C. Ingrey (sister), Messrs. F. and C. Starr (brothers), Messrs. C. and E. Perkiss (nephews), Mrs. A. Law (niece), Mr. J. Janeway (brother-in-law), Mesdames J. Janeway, E. Minns and J. Webber (sisters-in-law), Mesdames H. Gentle, G. Reynolds and A. Covington (cousins), Mr. and Mrs. Crow, Mr. W.F. Conner (employer), Messrs. E. Matthews, A. Conder, H. Covington, D. Bonfield, F. Bonfield and D. Kirbyshire (fellow workmen).'

31st July 1942 - Mrs Emily Pettengell of *'Laburnam Cottage'*

Feb 1943 - H Newell at Rickmansworth

'We regret to announce the death at the early age of 53 years of Mr. H. Newell, eldest son of the late Mr. and Mrs. M. Newell of Guilden Morden, and well known in district as the blacksmith family. Mr. and Mrs. Newell lived at the 'Six Bells', but carried on the smithy business also at Wrestlingworth, coming later to live at the 'Chequers' which adjoined the shop. Mrs. Newell was the daughter of the late Mr. and Mrs. Barnes of Cockayne Hatley, who were organists at the church. Mr H. Newell who has one son, served in the last war.'

5th April 1943 - Mrs Ellen Gentle

'The funeral of Mrs. Ellen Gentle, whose death occurred at a nursing home on April 5th, took place on 9th inst. The service was held in St. Bene't's Church, Cambridge, and was conducted by the Rev. J. Cobham, who also officiated at the interment at Guilden Morden Cemetery. On the plain oak coffin was the simple cross from her son Flight-Lieut. Sidney J. Gentle, who is on service in the East 'In loving memory of my dearest mother, from her devoted son Sidney, R.I.P.' The immediate mourners were: Mr. C. Lofts and Miss Edith Lofts (brother and niece), Mr. and Mrs G. Freestone (brother-in-law and sister), Mr. and Mrs. H. Gentle (brother-in-law and sister-in-law), Mrs. Peal (sister-in-law), Mr. Carter (brother-in-law), Mr. and Mrs. Moule (brother-in-law and sister-in-law), Mrs. Saville (sister-in-law), Miss Ada Gentle (sister-in-law), Mrs. K. Chapman (sister-in-law).'

3rd June 1943 - Mrs Emma Walker at North Brook End

'We record the passing of Mrs. Emma Walker widow of Mr. J. Walker, whose death occurred at her home at North Brook End, Steeple Morden on Thursday June 3rd, at the ripe old age of 82. During her long life she had won many friends by her faithful service, and kindly disposition, and many will recall her helpfulness in time of need. In her active days she was a faithful attendant at the Parish Church, and still remained a member of the Mothers' Union. The funeral service conducted by the vicar Rev. Ll.G.S. Price was held on Monday June 7th. The principal mourners were: Messrs. A. and F. Walker (sons), Mrs. F. Izzard and Mrs. C. Stewart (daughters), Messrs. W. and D. Thompson (brothers), Mrs. A. and Mrs F. Walker (daughters-in-law), Mr. F. Izzard and Mr. C. Stewart (sons-in-law), Mrs. A. and Mrs W. Foxon (grand-daughters)., Mr. W.J. Thompson, and Mr. and Mrs. E. Thompson (nephews and nieces), Mrs. Holton and Mrs. Foxon.'

5th June 1943 - Miss Mary Mudge

'We regret to record the passing of Miss Mary Mudge whose death occurred on Saturday June 5th at the age of 74. Since making her home with her sister, Mrs. J. Levy, the deceased had made many friends in the village, and her painful illness had evoked the sympathy of all who knew her. The funeral service at the Congregational Church on Thursday last week was conducted by the Rev. H.F. Hawkes. The principal mourners were Mrs. J. Levy and Mrs. Abbott (sisters), Mr. and Mrs. Mudge (brother and sister-in-law), Miss Levy and Miss King, and the Misses E. and B. Levy.'

31st August 1943 - Mrs Elizabeth Rowland

'In the passing of Mrs. Elizabeth Rowland, widow of the late Mr. Simeon Rowland of High Street, the village has lost another old and respected inhabitant. Her death, at the age of 88, took place on August 31st at the home of her daughter, Mrs. A. Starr where she had lived the last eight years. Though confined to bed practically all the time, she had borne her weakness with great courage and fortitude. She had been a member of the Congregational Church for many years, and a regular attendant at the services as long as she was able. The funeral service at the Congregational Church on Saturday was conducted by the Rev. H.F. Hawkes. The principal mourners were: Mrs. J. Janeway, Mrs. A. Starr, Mrs. J. Webber and Mrs. F. Mimms (daughters), Mrs. A. Cole (sister), Mr. J. Janeway and Mr. J. Webber (sons-in-law), Mr. H. Janeway and Mr. S. Starr (grandsons), Mrs. H. Janeway, Mrs. A. Baulk and Miss D. Starr (grand-daughters), Mrs. G. Reynolds, Mrs. H. Gentle and Mrs. A. Covington (nieces).'

6th Oct 1943 - Canon Arthur Lukyn Williams

'The death occurred on Wednesday of last week at the age of 90 of Canon Arthur Lukyn Williams, M.A., D.D., honorary Canon of Ely since 1912 and a former vicar of Guilden Morden. It is 24 years since Canon Lukyn retird at Guilden Morden, after a Ministry in the Parish of 24 years. He leaves a son and a daughter, the former being vicar of Nutfield, while another son was killed in the last war. Canon Williams had a distinguished ecclesiastical career. Educated at Haileybury and Jesus College, Cambridge, he was Prin-

cipal of Moore Theological College, Sydney, N.S.W., from 1878 to 1884. From 1891 to 1895 he was head of the London Mission of the London Jews' Society, and from 1911 to 1915 Warburton Lecturer at Lincoln's Inn. From 1914 to 1928 he was Warden of the Central Society of Sacred Study in the Diocese of Ely. Canon Williams was the author of many religious books. On Tuesday last a number of the villagers attended at the Parish Church to say farewell to their old vicar, whose remains had been brought from Nutfield, Surrey, for interment. The service was conducted by the present vicar the Rev. Ll G S Price, M.A. assisted by the Rev. C.A. Smith of Tamworth (an old village boy and one-time pupil of the late vicar). Mr. Price spoke of the talents of Dr. Williams, which had been used for the good of the church and spiritual help of the people, not only of the parish but in the world outside, where his book had been of help to many unable to hear his voice. The last of these was published within six years of his death. During the service Dr. William's favourite hymn 'Souls of men, why will ye scatter' was sung. Miss Price, L.R.A.M. was at the organ and played appropriate music.'

10th October 1943 - William George Levy at Guilden Morden, poultry farmer

19th November 1943 - Mrs Ada Slater at *'Morden House'*

1st December 1943 - Edward Thompson at Guilden Morden
'There was a fatal accident at Guilden Morden on Wednesday morning, when Mr. Edward Thompson, 48 years old, general labourer, of High Street, Guilden Morden, was killed when his cycle was in collision with a car. The driver of the car involved was Mr. H. Matthews, of Steeple Morden. Mr. Thompson was coming out of Church Street, and Mr. Matthews was proceeding towards Wrestlingworth when the collision took place and we understand that death was almost instantaneous. An inquest was held at Guilden Morden yesterday (Thursday).

The funeral of the late Mr. E. Thompson whose tragic death occurred last week, took place on Saturday. A short service conducted by the Congregational Minister the Rev. H.F. Hawkes was held in the home of deceased's sister, Mrs. T. Dowdy. The principal mourners were:- Mrs. T. Dowdy, Mrs. Manning (sisters), Mrs. A. Thompson (sister-in-law), Mr. T. Dowdy (brother-in-law), Mr. G. and Miss M. Izzard (nephew and niece), Mr. W. and Mr. D. Thompson (cousins).'

'An inquest was held on Thursday last on Mr. Edward Thompson, High Street, Guilden Morden, who was killed the previous day when riding his cycle, and coming into collision with a car at the junction of Church Street and Trap Road. The inquiry was conducted by the Deputy Coroner for Cambs. (Mr. V.O. Cade), Mr. Reginald Hartley of Royston represented the driver of the car, and P.S. Dean of Melbourn represented the police. George Sarl Woodage of Abington Pigotts Road, Litlington, said that at 7.45 a.m. on Wednesday he was cycling to work with deceased. Deceased had no lights on his cycle. They were proceeding out of Church Street and were going to turn right into Trap Road. Deceased was riding about four feet ahead of him and had made a half right turn when the front of his

cycle collided with the near front side of a car proceeding along Trap Road.. Witness estimated the speed of the car, which was carrying lights, at 25m.p.h., and Thompson was dead when witness went to where he was lying in the road. The hearing and eyesight of deceased, a single man, were both good. Answering Mr. Hartley, witness said their speed was about 5 m.p.h. He first saw a car when it was three feet away from deceased, and the driver had no chance of pulling up. The car gave no warning of its approach. The driver of the car concerned, Horace Archer Matthews, farmer, Station Road, Steeple Morden, said that he was proceeding along Trap Road, and when approaching Church Street junction he saw the cyclist about five yards in front of him and at the centre of the road. Witness pulled over sharp to the right to avoid the cyclist but before he could stop the cyclist struck the car. Witness said that he thought the cyclist was giving him the right of the road and that was why he pulled over to the right. The car was practically stopped when the cyclist struck it. The cyclist was carrying no lights, but the car was using sidelights and headlights. Answering Sergt. Dean, witness said he was right on the corner when he saw the cyclist. He knew the road well and was travelling at 10 m..h. He did not sound his hooter when approaching the corner. P.C. Cornwall (Guilden Morden) said he was called to the accident at 7.50 a.m. The cycle was lying one foot from the left-hand wing of the car, and deceased was lying in the road three feet away from his cycle. He was bleeding freely from the head, and also had a compound fracture of the right leg. The cycle had no front light, and the rear light was out of order. The brakes were in order. The width of the road at the point of collision was 32 feet, and the road was slippery. Lighting-up time ended at 8.12 a.m. that morning. Summing up, the Deputy Coroner said that the deceased contributed to his own death by not carrying lights on his cycle. He returned a verdict of "Accidental death" the cause of death being a fractured skull. The Coroner, Mr. Hartley and Sergt. Dean all expressed sympathy with the relatives.'

20th December 1943 - George Watts at Guilden Morden
'By the death of Mr. George Watts of Townsend, which took place at his home on Monday December 20th, the village loses another of its older inhabitants. Despite his 89 years, he had remained quite active and energetic and was a familiar figure about the village. To those who had seen him a short time previously his rather sudden passing came as a shock. He leaves four sons and five daughters, having lost one son in the 1914-18 war. The funeral service, conducted by the Rev. H.F. Hawkes, was held at the Congregational Church on Friday 24th December. The family mourners were:- E.H.F. and T. Watts (sons), Mrs. T. Hyde, Mrs. G. Izzard, Mrs. L. Luke, Miss F. Watts and Mrs. S. Stockwell (daughters), Messrs T. Hyde, G. Izzard, Luke S. Stockwell (sons-in-law), Mrs. A. Evans, Mrs. S. Worboys, Miss J. Watts (grand-daughters), A. & S. Watts (grand-sons), Miss R. Potton.'

26th December 1943 - Thomas Price Keightley, baker retired
'We regret to record the death of Mr. Thomas Price Keightley, who passed away on Sunday, December 26th, at the great age of 83 years. Deceased, who was a native of Melbourn, spent most of his working years in London, and came to reside in the village five-and-a-half years ago. His kindly disposition soon gained him many friends and

together with his wife enjoyed many of the amenities of village life. While able, he was a regular attendant at the Congregational Church, and almost his last appearance in public was at a service there. Many will feel his loss most keenly and the greatest sympathy is felt for his widow. The funeral service at the Congregational Church on Thursday December 30th was conducted by the Rev. H.F. Hawkes. The principal mourners were:- Mrs. T. Keightley (widow), Mr. and Mrs. G. Lindsay (son-in-law and daughter), Sgt. F. Keightley R.A.F. (nephew), Mrs. Johnson (niece), Mr. and Mrs. Reading (grand-niece and nephew), Mr. and Mrs. F. Chilvers (Norwich), Mr. B. Moore (London), Mr. and Mrs. J. Humphries (London), Mr. Howard Davies (Hendon).'

29th December 1943 - Mrs Agnes Ann Matthews

'After a long period of weakness and disability during which she was lovingly cared for by members of her family, Mrs. Agnes Matthews, wife of the late Mr. W. Matthews of Church Street passed away on Wednesday 29th December 1943, at the advanced age of 75 years. A native of Guilden Morden, Mrs. Matthews was well-known and respected by all. Many have reason to remember her neighbourly help in times of need. She had a life-long attachment to the Congregational Church, and her family of three sons and five daughters had all passed through the Sunday School. The funeral service, on New Year's Day, was conducted by Rev. H.F. Hawkes with Mr. O. Kaye at the organ. The principal mourners were: Mr. J. Matthews, Sgt. Major V. Matthews, Mr H. Matthews (sons), Mrs. A. Thompson, Mrs. A. Hawkins, Mrs. M. Bowen, Mrs. W. Saunders (daughters), Mr. A. Hawkins (son-in-law), Miss J. Thompson (grand-daughter), Mr. Dennis Thompson , Messrs. B. and J. Bowen (grand-sons), Mrs Beedell and Miss R. Merrill (nieces), Mr. E. Matthews (brother-in-law), Mr. F. Johnson.'

30th December 1943 - Mrs Fanny Harris at Church Street

'The death occurred on Thursday December 30th of Mrs. E. Harris, wife of Mr. E. Harris of Church Street after a short illness at the age of 77 years. Though not a native of Guilden Morden, deceased had lived in the village for the greater part of her life, and was well known in the district. The funeral service at the Parish Church was conducted by the Vicar, Rev. Ll.G.S. Price. The principal mourners were: Mr. E. Harris (husband), Mr. and Mrs. A. Harris (brother-in-law and sister-in-law), Mrs. G. Gentle (niece), Mr. T. Harris (nephew), Mrs. Jenkins (Therfield)...'

6th February 1944 - Frederick Webb at High Street

'In the passing of Mr. F. Webb of High Street, whose death took place on Sunday 6th February, at the age of 91, the village has lost its oldest inhabitant. In earlier days he achieved fame as a well-digger and borer for water, and gained an extensive knowledge of local water supplies over a wide district. He had four sons, three of whom are living, one being in Australia, and two daughters. Three of his four grandsons are in the Forces, and he had three grand-daughters. The funeral took place on Wednesday 9th February. The Rev. H.F. Hawkes conducted a short service at the house. The principal mourners were: Messrs.

A. and E. Webb (sons), Mrs. G. Hart (daughter), Mrs. A. Webb (daughter-in-law), Mrs. A. Coole (niece), Mrs. Mence.'

8th Feb 1944 - Miss Elizabeth Ann Clarke at *'Saville House'*
'In the passing of Miss E.A. Clarke of 'Saville House', whose death took place at her home on Tuesday last week at the age of 86 years, the village loses an outstanding personality. In earlier days her boarding school was the beginning of learning for many little folk, and in some cases their children followed them and also learned to love and respect their gracious teacher. Many today remember her with gratitude and affection. She was a lifelong member of the Congregational Church, and for nearly forty years held the office of organist and choirmistress, where, by patience and perseverance in training, she brought a new insight into the beauty of sacred music to those who came under her tuition, and who still feel a debt of gratitude towards her. At the time of her death she was senior deacon of the church and for a number of years had held the office of treasurer. Although increasing weakness had latterly debarred her from taking an active part in church affairs she retained a keen interest in all its activities to the last. Given to hospitality, her home was always open to entertain visiting Ministers, Students and Missionary Deputations, and many will remember her as a gracious and charming hostess. The greatest sympathy is felt for her sister Mrs. A.A. Saunderson, the only surviving member of the family.

The funeral service at the Congregational Church on Friday February 11th was conducted by Rev. H.F. Hawkes. During a short address the Pastor spoke with sincere affection of the place the deceased had held in the hearts of those present, and of the loyal Christian service she had rendered to the church. The principal mourners were:- Mr. A.G. Worboys, Mrs. F. Thurlbourn, Mr. Percy Worboys, Mrs. S. Randall, Mrs. F.W.P. Hunt, Mrs. Coxall, Mr. A. Saunderson, Mr. A. and Miss E. Worboys, Mr. E. Matthews and Mr. W.J. Gentle (fellow deacons).'

21st February 1944 - Miss Rosa Hemmersley at *'Morden House'*

23rd February 1944 - George Thomas Reynolds at the *'Chestnut Tree'*
'News of the sudden passing of Mr. G.T. Reynolds of the 'Chestnut Tree' on Thursday of last week, came as a great shock to the village. Deceased, apparently in normal health, had carried on with his work as usual on Wednesday but was taken ill during the night, and quickly passed away. He was 72 years of age. A native of Ashwell, he had resided in the village for some forty years. Coming, in the first place, as head groom to the late Mr. W.A. Sandeman, of Morden House, he later had charge of the famous prize-winning herd of Poll Angus Cattle, and doubtless played a great part in their steady rise to fame. During the last few years he had been the licensee of the 'Chestnut Tree'. The funeral service on Saturday last at the Parish Church was conducted by the Vicar, Rev. Ll.G.S. Price. The family mourners were Mr. and Mrs. G. Reynolds (son and daughter-in-law), Mr. and Mrs. C. Reynolds (brother and sister-in-law), Mr. O.J. Reynolds (brother), Mrs. F. Randall, Mrs. L. Dennis (niece). Others present were:- Mrs. H. Gentle, Mrs. A. Covington, Mrs. G. Pettengell, Mr. Meakin, Mr. A.L. Izzard, , Mr. O. Kaye...'

29th February 1944 - George Pettengell of *'Laburnum Cottage'*, smallholder

'We record with regret the death of Mr. G. Pettengell of 'Laburnum Cottage', which took place at his home on Tuesday February 29th, after a short illness at the age of 74 years. The funeral service at the Parish Church on Friday March 3rd, was conducted by the Vicar Rev. Ll G S Price, assisted by Rev. H.F. Hawkes, Congregational Minister. The principal mourners were:- Mr. and Mrs. W. Pettengell (brother and sister-in-law), Mrs. Pooley (niece), Mr. H. Barton (brother-in-law), Mrs. Bullock, Mrs. Mence...'

13th April 1944 - Louisa Smalls, retired nurse at *'Morden House'*

28th April 1944 - Miss Cecilia Masters of *'Willowdale'* at Cambridge

'We regret to record the death of Miss C.A. Masters of Willowdale, Guilden Morden, which took place at Cambridge on Friday April 28th at the age of 75 years. A member of an old and respected family she had lived most of her life in the village and had kept the old home in existence since the death of her parents. As long as her health permitted she had been a regular adherent of the Congregational Church and a faithful member of the working party. Following an old family custom the funeral service was held at the Parish Church on Wednesday May 3rd, conducted by the Vicar, Rev. Ll.G.S. Price. The principal mourners were Messrs. T. and C.A. Masters (brothers), Mrs. B. Hall (sister), Mrs. J. Tompkins and Miss Sheila Hall (nieces), Mr. Geoff Hall (nephew), Miss M. Conder.'

9th May 1944 - Alfred William Essam at the *'Six Bells'*

4th August 1944 - Mrs Selina Dellar at the *'Brickfields'*

'The death of Mrs. Selina Dellar of Brickyard, Guilden Morden, took place on Friday last week, at the home of her sister, with whom she had lived for the last 12 years. Mrs. Dellar had been in failing health for a long time which was borne with courage and fortitude. She was 79 years of age and was born in the village. The funeral took place on Monday at the Parish Church, the Vicar Rev. Ll.G.S. Price officiating. The family mourners were:- Messrs. W. and A. Covington (brothers), Mrs. A. Bonnett, Mrs. F. Starr and Mrs. G. Bird (sisters), Mrs. G. Covington and Mrs. W. Covington (sisters-in-law), Mr. F. Starr (brother-in-law), Mrs. Dowdy and Mrs. Ingrey...'

17th August 1944 - Mrs Sarah Ann Worboys at Cambridge

'The passing of Mrs. S.A. Worboys, which occurred at Cambridge on August 17th, at the age of 85 years, removes another link with a former generation. Mrs. Worboys was the widow of Mr. Charles Worboys (at one time a farmer at Bourn). She was a native of Guilden Morden, as was her husband, and both were held in the highest esteem by all who knew them. They were married at the Congregational Church in 1881 and have always maintained a keen and kindly interest in its welfare. The funeral service at the Congregational Church on Monday was conducted by the Rev. H.F. Hawkes. Mr. O. Kaye was at the organ. The chief mourners were:- Mr. F. Arundel (son-in-law, adopted), Miss Jean Arundel (grand-daughter), Mr. E. Matthews (brother-in-law), Mr. and Mrs. A. Kaye

(brother-in-law and sister-in-law), Mr. F. Clarke, Mrs. Cross, Miss Gentle, Mrs. Barratt, Mrs. Lawford (nieces), Mr. O. Kaye (nephew), Miss Daphne Kaye, Mrs. Furness (Cambridge), Mrs. Crow (Bourn), Mr. Crown (Sidcup).'

10th September 1944 - Mrs Jane Levy at Guilden Morden

24th September 1944 - Mrs Emily Jane Worboys of *'Avenel Terrace'*
'We record the death of Mrs. Emily Jane Worboys, wife of Mr. Charles Worboys, of 2 Avenel Terrace, which occurred on Sunday September 24th at the age of 70 years. She had been a great sufferer for a long period, and especially during the later stages of her illness, but all her sufferings were patiently borne. The funeral service at the Congregational Church on Wednesday September 27th was conducted by the Rev. H F Hawkes, Mr. O. Kaye presiding at the organ. The principal mourners were:- Mr. C. Worboys (husband), Mrs. Clover, Mrs. Simmons, Mrs. Ball and Miss Willmott (sisters), Messrs. Charles and George Willmott (brothers), Mrs. Pettengell.'

19th October 1944 - Mrs Annie Florence Prior, evacuee at Guilden Morden

23rd December 1944 - William Scott at Linton
'We record the death of Mr. William Scott, who passed away at Linton on Saturday Dec 23rd, at the age of 78 years. The funeral service at the cemetery was conducted by Rev. H.F.Hawkes. The principal mourners were Messrs. J. and H. Watts and W. and G. Scott (sons), Mrs. Horsley and Mrs. Adams (Daughters), Mrs. L. Gentle (granddaughter), Mr. H. Horsley (grandson), Mrs. J. Watts, Mrs. H. Watts and Mrs. G. Scott (daughters-in-law), Mr. W.F. Connor (a former employer) and other friends were present at the cemetery.'

8th January 1945 - Miss Margaret Elizabeth Hollis at *'Morden House'*

10th February 1945 - Henry James Harper at Harston, retired baker

28th February 1945 - Mrs Mary Harper at Harston

25th June 1945 - Signaller Bernard Frank Bonfield in Germany
'The sad news received during this week-end by Mr. and Mrs. F. Bonfield of the 'Black Horse', of the death of their son, Signaller B.F. Bonfield, as a result of accidental gunshot wounds, seems doubly hard now that hostilities are over. 'Bernie', as he was always known in the village, was a quiet unassuming lad, and a general favourite. He was formerly employed by Messrs. A. & J. Worboys. The greatest sympathy is felt for his parents and all members of the family in their great loss.'

6th July 1945 - Miss Sylvia Joan Leete at Hitchin

'We record the death of Private Sylvia Joan Leete, A.T.S., second daughter of Mr. and Mrs. C. Leete, of London Road, Baldock, and formerly of Guilden Morden, which took place at Hitchin on Friday July 6th at the age 25 years, after a severe illness,patiently borne. The funeral service at the Congregational Church on Tuesday was conducted by the Rev. H.F. Hawkes. The family morners were:- Mr. and Mrs. C.W. Leete (father and mother), Mr. and Mrs. I. Leete (brother and sister-in-law), Mrs. H. Langton and Miss Marie Leete (sisters), Messrs. Philip and Rober Leete (brothers), Mt. and Mrs. W. Rule, Mr. and Mrs. H.S. Rule, Mrs. H.Westrope, Mr. D. Thompson (uncles and aunts), Mr. E.J. Westrope, Miss B. Westrope and Miss E. Rule (cousins).'

20th July 1945 - Miss Martha Long at Guilden Morden

'The death occurred on Friday July 20th of Miss Martha Long, of High Street, at the advanced age of 89. She was one of the two remaining members of the family of the late Mr and Mrs John Long, who were well known to a former generation. Deceased, who had given faithful service to a number of families in her active days, was much respected by those whom she served. The funeral service at the Congregational Church on Wednesday July 25th, was conducted by the Rev. H F Hawkes, Mrs L Mence presiding at the organ. The principal mourners were Miss P Long (sister), Mrs G Pettengell and Mrs J East (cousins), and other relatives, Mrs J Sale (Letchworth, a former employer).'

19th August 1945 - Gunner John Edward Davis

'We regret to record the death of still another of our fine young men while a prisoner in Japanese hands, Gunner John Edward Davis, R.A. Gunner Davis , who was 29, made his home with his sister, Mrs. Steel, after the death of his mother in 1985. He was well known and very popular among the young people. Gunner Davis had been a P.O.W. since the fall of Singapore, and according to official information he passed away in Thailand on Aug 19th 1945, after an attack of dysentery and malaria. The sincerest sympathy will be extended to Mr. and Mrs. Steel in their bereavement.'

12th November 1945 - Mrs Clara Hall at Chalkdell Hospital, Hitchin

1st December 1945 - Mrs Emma Clements at Guilden Morden

24th January 1946 - Mrs Flora Wright of Church Lane

'The funeral of Mrs F Wright was conducted by the Rev. A F Gardiner at the Parish Church, Mr O Kaye presiding at the organ. The principal mourners were Mr Aubrey Wright (grandson), Mrs A Elbourn and Miss M Wright (grand-daughters), Mr A Elbourn, Mrs W J Thompson and Mrs G Hitch, Mrs A Wright (daughters-in-law).'

15th Feb 1946 - Henry Grocott of 'The Dene'

22nd May 1946 - William Izzard at Guilden Morden

30th May 1946 - Mrs Sarah Thompson of High Street, Knapwell

9th June 1946 - Mrs Lilla Covington of High Street

10th December 1946 - David Thompson of Ashwell Road

'His Last Load Home. In the passing of Mr David Thompson of 6 Council Cottages, whose death took place on Tuesday of last week, at the age of 83 years, the village loses another of its old and respected inhabitants. He found his greatest pleasure in his work, and was a craftsman of no mean ability. Starting as a shock boy at Rectory Farm, when he was five years old, he took part in every harvest there for the next 51 years, first with the late Mr J G Johnson, and later with Mr F Hunt. After this he worked under various masters, and latterly, with his son, he continued with the work he really loved, finishing this year with an unbroken record of 77 consecutive harvests. The funeral service at the Parish Church on Saturday was conducted by the Vicar, Rev A F Gardiner. Mr O Kaye presiding at the organ. The principal mourners were: Messrs E and F Thompson (sons), Miss A Thompson (daughter), Mrs E and Mrs F Thompson (daughters-in-law), Mr A Dellar (son-in-law), Mr W and Mr J Thompson (brothers), Mr H and Mr S Thompson (grandsons), Miss Audrey Thompson (grand-daughter), Mr and Mrs F Izzard, Mr F and Mr E Thompson (Steeple Morden), Mr A Thompson and Mr L Shelton (Knapwell), Mr H Gentle, Mr G Moule, Mrs Dowdy and Miss G Thompson (nephews and nieces), Mr A Pearce (friend), Miss S Thompson. Mrs A Dellar and Mr D Thompson were unable to attend.'

10th January 1947 - Thomas Masters at Guilden Morden

28th August 1947 - Henry John Horsley at Guilden Morden

6th September 1947 - Arthur Edward Law of *'Dove Cottage'*

'The sudden passing of Mr Arthur Edward Law at the age of 51, came as a great shock to his friends as it did to the whole village. Deceased, who was apparently in fair health, had been working as usual on Saturday Aug 30th, feeling unwell later in the evening, he went to Dr Moynihan at Ashwell who sent him to Fairfield Hospital, where he underwent an operation. His recovery from this seemed satisfactory, but complications set in, and he passed away on Wednesday last week. Deceased leaves a widow, two sons and two daughters, for whom the greatest sympathy is felt. The funeral service at the Parish Church was conducted by the Vicar, Rev A F Gardiner, Mr O Kaye presiding at the organ. The principal mourners were Mrs Law (widow), Messrs F and D Law (sons), Mrs F Kirbyshire and Miss Joyce Law (daughters), Mrs Sullivan and Miss M Law (sisters), Mr F Kirbyshire (son-in-law), Mr and Mrs F Starr (father and mother-in-law), Mrs C Ingrey and Mrs C Bird (aunts), Mrs G Watson and Mrs T Williams (cousins), Mr S Kirby (employer).'

28th September 1947 - Mary Ann Long at Linton

3rd December 1947 - Alfred Haylock, at Guilden Morden, smallholder

23rd February 1948 - Walter Covington of the *'Pear Tree'* at Guilden Morden
'By the death of Mr Walter Covington of the 'Pear Tree' Guilden Morden on Monday 23rd February at the age of 75 years, the village loses another familiar figure in everyday life. 'Nipper', as he was known to his associates, spent most of his working days at Rectory Farm, and the various employers whom he served all found him a loyal and trustworthy workman. Following his father-in-law, the late Mr G Izzard, as licensee of the 'Pear Tree', the two families have held the licence of the house some fifty-seven years. Having enjoyed good health for most of his life, an operation last year, and the weakness following, seemed especially hard to bear, but his natural patience proved his greatest asset. The funeral service at the Parish Church on Thursday February 26th, was conducted by the Vicar, the Rev A F Gardiner. The principal mourners were: Mrs Covington (widow), Mr and Mrs J Peckett, Mr and Mrs W Rosendale, Mr and Mrs J Woods (daughters and sons-in-law), Mr A Covington (brother), Mrs F Starr, Mrs G Bird (sisters), Mrs H Thompson, Mrs A Mynott, Mr and Mrs R Rosendale, Mrs R Roberts, Misses Elsie and Mary Peckett (grandchildren), Mr A Covington (nephew), Mrs G Watson, Mrs A Law, Mrs T Williams (nieces), Mr and Mrs G Izzard (brother and sister-in-law).'

9th March 1948 - Violet Eva Mackarsie at Guilden Morden
'We regret to record the death of Mrs W J Mackarsie, which took place at her home o Tuesday March 9th at the age of fifty-four years. Having been evacuated from London during the war, she had settled in the village and her genial disposition won her many friends in the community. Although she had been in poor health for some time, her sudden passing, the result of a seizure, came as a shock to the village. The funeral service at the Congregational Church on Thursday March 11th was conducted by the Rev H F Hawkes, Mr O Kaye presiding at the organ. The principal Mourners were: Mr W J Mackarsie (husband), Mr Donald Mackarsie (son), Mr G Neale (brother), Mrs H P Day (sister), Miss A Mackarsie and Mrs G Neale (sister-in-law), Mr H P Day (brother-in-law), Miss E Levy and Miss B Levy (friends).'

14th March 1948 - Mrs Eliza Ann Sinclair Izzard of High Street at Hayes, Middlesex
'We regret to record the death of Mrs A J L Izzard of High Street who passed away at her daughter's house at Hayes, Middlesex, on Sunday March 14th at the age of 71. Mrs Izzard had been in poor health for some time. The funeral service at the Congregational Church on Wednesday March 17th was conducted by Rev H F Hawkes, with Mr O Kaye at the organ. The principal mourners were: Mr A J L Izzard (husband), Mr A Izzard (son), Mrs Taylor and Mrs Roberts (daughters), Mrs A Izzard (daughter-in-law), Mr Roberts and Mr Taylor (sons-in-law), Miss M Morris (niece), and Mrs F Izzard.'

6th April 1948 - Mr Wilfred Izzard of 'Lyncroft'
'We regret to record the passing of Mr Wilfred Izzard of 'Lyncroft' whose death occurred on Tuesday April 6th at the age of 71. The deceased was a native of the village and was well known in the district, and for the last few years had been in the employ of Mr E W Pepper. Up to the end of last year he had continued in regular work and his illness was of short duration. The funeral service at the Congregational Church was conducted by the Minister, Rev H F Hawkes. In the absence of the organist Mr O Kaye, through illness, Mrs F Chamberlain accompanied the singing of the hymns. The principal mourners were: Mr C Izzard (son), Mrs R Worboys, Mrs S Worboys (daughters), Miss P Worboys (grand-daughter), Messrs R and S Worboys (sons-in-law), Mrs C Izzard (daughter-in-law), Messrs A and G Izzard (brothers), Mrs W Covington (sister), Mrs G Izzard (sister-in-law), Mr and Mrs J Worboys (sister-in-law and brother-in-law), Mrs S Bryant (niece).'

21st April 1948 - Mrs Sarah Ann Covington of the 'Pear Tree'
'The tragic passing of Mrs W Covington of the 'Pear Tree' on Wednesday April 21st at the age of 78 years came as a shock to the whole village. Since the death of her husband in February last she had carried on in her usual way, and on Monday April 19th set out to attend the magistrates court at Arrington for the purpose of the transfer of the licence in her own name. On arrival there she was found in a state of collapse. Assistance was obtained and she was brought home and medical help obtained, but in spite of everything that could be done she passed away in the early hours of Wednesday morning. She will be missed by many who have known her during her long residence at the 'Pear Tree' for her cheerful manner and ready help whenever needed. The funeral service was conducted by the Vicar, the Rev A F Gardiner, Miss Gardiner at the organ. The principal mourners were: Mrs J Peckett, Mrs W Rosendale, Mrs J Woods (daughters), Messrs A and G Izzard (brothers), Messrs J Peckett, W Rosendale, J Woods (sons-in-law), Mrs F Blair and Mrs G Izzard (sisters-in-law), Mr H Thompson, Mr and Mrs A Mynott, Mr H Rosendale, Mr and Mrs H Roberts, the Misses Elsie, Mary and Hetty Peckett (grand-daughters), Mrs G Watson, Mrs T Williams, Mrs A Law, Mr H Izzard, Mrs Eccleshall, Mr A Covington, Mr and Mrs C Izzard, Mrs Arthur Kirbyshire, Mrs Albert Kirbyshire, Mr and Mrs H Williams, Mrs E Waldock (nephews and nieces), Mr W Dowton and Miss D Woods, Mrs E Ingrey, Mrs King and Mrs F Walker.'

24th April 1948 - Cecil Wynn Leete at Baldock
'The death of Mr C W Leete of London Road, Baldock on Saturday April 24th, was keenly felt by all who knew him. His Marriage to Miss Nettie Rule made a link with the village where he lived after the 1914-18 war, until his removal to Baldock. He was an extremely active member and first secretary of the Guilden Morden branch of the British Legion, and in November of last year unveiled the names of the fallen in the 1939-45 war, and which had been inscribed on the memorial, among which were the names of his nephew and dearly loved daughter. Following the cremation at Golder's Green the ashes were interred on the grave of his daughter in the cemetery at Guilden Morden on Thursday last, the committal service being conducted by the Rev H F Hawkes, Congregational minister. The principal

mourners were: Mrs C W Leete widow), Messrs Philip and Robert Leete (sons), Mrs Langton and Miss Marie Leete (daughters), Messrs W Rule, Mrs H S Rule, Mrs H J Westrope (sisters-in-law), Mrs T Bath, Mr F W Murfitt, Mr A J Worboys, Miss E Worboys, Mrs A Kaye, Mr and Mrs O Kaye...'

9th October 1948 - Mrs Evelyn Mary Pearce of Queensland, Australia

'The ashes of the late Mrs H Pearce, who died recently in Australia, were interred in the grave of her parents, the late Mr and Mrs D Clarke, at the cemetery on Saturday afternoon. Mrs Pearce was the wife of Mr H Pearce of South Queensland, Australia and formerly of Wendy. The ceremony was conducted by the Vicar, the Rev A F Gardiner. Those present were: Mr and Mrs F Clarke (brother and sister-in-law), Geoffrey Clarke (nephew), Mr and Mrs H Barnes (sister and brother-in-law), Mr G and Miss Parsons (brother-in-law and niece), Mr A Izzard and Mr E Matthews (uncles), Miss Morris (cousin)...'

10th October 1948 - Mr Charles Murfitt

'We regret to record this week the death of Mr Charles Murfitt, a well-known and respected figure in the district. The death took place on Sunday October 10th, within a few days of his 80th birthday. The funeral took place at the Congregational Chapel yesterday.'

Charles Murfitt was the first Clerk of the Parish Council, and then Chairman until 1945 when he retired.

25th December 1948 - James Thompson at Knapwell

31st December 1948 - James Barker Winders at Guilden Morden, retired farmer

22nd January 1949 - Mrs Amy Lilley of Silver Street

'The death occurred on Thursday last week of Mrs A Lilley, widow of Mr J Lilley of Silver Street, at the age of 69 years. Deceased had been a great sufferer over a long period, and will be greatly missed by her family of three sons and two daughters, who are left to mourn their loss. The funeral service at the Parish Church on Saturday last wad conducted by the vicar, Rev D Murray Greenhalgh M.A., Mr O Kaye being the organist. The principal mourners were: Messrs Gordon, Charles and Cecil Lilley (sons), Mrs W Watts and Mrs H Hart (daughters), Mrs Gordon Lilley and Mrs Charles Lilley (daughters-in-law), Mr H Hart (son-in-law), Mr Leslie Harris.'

2nd March 1949 - Alfred Bonfield of *'Avenel Place'* at Welwyn

'The death took place at Welwyn on March 2nd, after a short illness, of Mr Alfred Bonfield, better known to residents of Guilden Morden, of which village he was a native, as 'Shepherd' Bonfield. He was 71 years of age and died at the home of his niece, Mrs Ward. For a number of years he was employed by Worboys Brothers. The funeral took place at Guilden Morden on Saturday last and was conducted by the Vicar, Rev. Greenhalgh. The principal mourners were: Mr Frank Bonfield (brother), Mr and Mrs Ward of Welwyn, Mrs S Thompson, Mrs C Purkiss, Mr G Cole, Mrs W Conder and Mrs C Watson.'

22 March 1949 - Samuel John Gentle of Guilden Morden at Chesterton
Samuel was buried in Guilden Morden Cemetery on 26th March.

16th Jul 1949 - Llewellyn Griffith Price of Ipswich, retired clergyman
(The following obituary appeared in the Guilden Morden Parish Magazine in August 1949)
'The Revd. Ll.G.S. Price, M.A., Vicar of Guilden Morden from 1919-1945, died at his house at Ipswich on July 16th. Educated at Trinity College, Dublin, Mr. Price was ordained in Manchester in 1889. He spent many years in the mission field in India, and was always keenly interested in the missionary work of the church. Returning to England in 1918, he became Vicar of this parish until his retirement, serving as Rural Dean of Shingay from 1933-1941.His faithful ministry in this parish will be long remembered by many to whom he proved himself a pastor and friend. An able preacher and a genial personality, he did much both here and abroad for which his friends are grateful to God. Failing health brought about his retirement, and in his closing years he was greatly helped by the care and devotion of his daughter. Our sympathetic thoughts are with her and with his sons at this time.*

The funeral service took place in our church on July 19th, previously to interment at the Guilden Morden cemetery. The hymns sung were 'Hark, hark, my soul' and 'O for a closer walk.' Mr. O. Kaye was at the organ. An address was given by the Rev. M. de Courcy-Ireland, M.A., formerly Vicar of Litlington and Rural Dean of Shingay, who also officiated at the graveside. Prayers were said by the Revd. F.C. Clare, M.A., Vicar of Whaddon and Rural Dean of Shingay, and the lesson was read by the Revd. N.W. Hill, M.A., Precentor of St. Albans Abbey. A large number of friends and sympathisers was present, and floral tributes included those from the Parochial Church Council of Guilden Morden, and also from the Staff, Scholars and Managers of the village school. A muffled peal was rung on the evening of Tuesday, 19th July, under the direction of Mr. V. Leonard. On Sunday July 24th at all the services in church, commemoration was made of the life and work of Mr. Price. Grant him Thy peace, and let light perpetual shine upon him.'

26th December 1949 - Frances Lilla Kaye of Guilden Morden
Mrs Kaye was buried in Guilden Morden Cemetery on 29th December.

Chapter 5

Services and Amenities

Telephones

We are now so used to the availability of telephone communications, using land lines, mobiles and telephone over the internet, that it comes as a shock to realise that during the 1940's relatively few people had access to a telephone except by using a public call box. The telephone was first patented by Alexander Graham Bell in the USA in 1876. This was followed by the introduction of the first commercial telephone exchanges in 1878/79 on both sides of the Atlantic. Early telephones had only one opening for sound and the user alternately listened and spoke. The use of telephones expanded rapidly and by 1925, the Steeple Morden Exchange had been established for the villages of Steeple Morden, Guilden Morden, Litlington and Abington Pigotts.

The exchange was in a private house in Cheyney Street, Steeple Morden. Subscribers were listed in the Post Office Telephone Directory under the Cambridge Area.

In 1925 there were just ten entries for this exchange:–
'Steeple Morden 1' was in the name of Lily Matthews, the operator.

Other numbers included:
Steeple Morden 5 - Murfitt, Charles. Farmer, Tax Collector.
Steeple Morden 7 - Sandeman, W. A. Morden House.
Steeple Morden 8 - Saunderson, Miller Coal Merchant, Mill House.

By **1941**, the number of users on the Steeple Morden exchange had increased to forty eight. To allow for future growth a three digit number was used; all numbers started with a '2'. Thus Mr. Charles Murfitt's number became 205. Other Guilden Morden numbers included:

252 - Barrenger WG (JP). The Priory.
251 - Carter E. Hooks Mill (Ernest Carter).
212 - Connor WF. Farmer (Town Farm).
211 - Day HP PO (Harry Day at the Post Office).
203 - Fordham Hon. Mrs. JP Ringdale.
242 - Fordham, Russell.
210 - Fordham SH Farmer, Cheyneys Lodge, Ashwell.
(The Fordhams lived at Odsey, within the parish of Guilden Morden).
262 - Hayward, Joseph. Avenells.
264 - Kirby FH, Morden Hall (Frank Kirby).
232 - Lindsay GW. Baker, Confectioner (George Lindsay).

207 - Saunderson E Ltd. Miller, Coal Merchant, Mill House.
228 - Seeley AS. Windy Ridge.
259 - Still EH. The Cottage.
256 - Willcock, Winifred. Morden House.
(The 'Matron' in charge of the evacuated ladies nursing home).
249 - Worboys F & Sons. Builders (Frank Worboys).

By **1949** there were about eighty five subscribers listed on the Steeple Morden exchange. The numbering system was unchanged. Some new subscribers since 1941 included:

259 - Aldridge LC. The Cottage.
213 - Chitty Lt.Col. JW (MBE). Riversdale.
240 - Crittall MG. Rectory Farm.
240 - Davenport JW. Rectory Farm.
278 - Dennis F. Valley Farm.
266 - Dellar WG. High Street.
262 - Gordon Douglas. Avenels.
232 - Lindsay SH Baker, High Street (Sid Lindsay).
279 - Rule HS. The Bungalow.
240 - Saul TA. Rectory Farm.
256 - Thompson Douglas J. Morden House.

The telephone directory had advertisements, including one for the 'Hand-Microphone'.
Local calls on ordinary lines were charged at four different rates from 1d to 4d, depending on the distance between the sending and receiving exchanges, irrespective of the length of the call. Note there was a war surcharge of 15%.
Trunk calls were charged based on the duration of the call.
Personal calls. It was possible to book a trunk call to a specific person and the caller would only be charged for the time when he or she was put in touch with that person. It would be ideal now for telephoning call centres!
International calls. These were suspended during the war.
Overseas telegrams. These were subject to restrictions because of the war.
The time. The operator would tell the time for the cost of a local call.

Postal Services

The village Post Office was in Church Street. In the 1940's there were two collections a day from the post boxes in Church Street and on the corner of High Street and Buxtons Lane. Postage charges were calculated by weight. The 'inland letter' rate for letters weighing up to 2 oz was 2$^{1}/_{2}$d (1p) in 1941, increasing to 3d in 1949. For further details about the Post Office and the village postman – see Chapter 7.

Water Supply

In 1935 the Parish Council asked South Cambridgeshire Rural District Council for a piped supply to the village. Piped water reached the village in 1939, just in time for the ARP fire hydrants. However, it took several years to connect all the houses and then for individual houses to install internal plumbing systems.

".... now with regard to fresh drinking water and so on, you had a galvanised bucket, and that had a wooden lid on top of it. And you used to fill it up from the pump ..."
Marjorie Baker *(Oral History Recordings)*

Sewerage

There was no sewerage system in Guilden Morden during the 1940's. The main sewer was not laid until 1968, with most houses connected in 1969.

"....We had outside toilets. We did have a bath but no running water over the bath."
(Cynthia Worboys *(Oral History Recordings)*

"... the privy was up the garden, in the barn where you kept your coal and chopped sticks and done all sorts there."
Marjorie Baker *(Oral History Recordings)*

Electricity

The electricity supply reached the major part of village after the war. We are not sure of the precise date. Again, it would have taken some time to wire the houses, so full electrification was a gradual process. Some of the larger houses were beginning to have some rooms fitted in early 1939, as can be seen from the letter shown here. Enquiries were made by the Parish Council in 1946 to the Beds, Cambs & Hunts Electricity Co. (later merged into Eastern Electricity) about lighting the village streets. In 1947 the same company was asked when the electricity supply would be extended to Great Green.

"....We had no hot water on at all, and no electricity when we first moved down (to New Road) *I think, but later on the electricity was fitted.... We used to have oil lamps and candles... I can remember sitting round the table with an oil lamp and hitting your hair, and it all used to cling to the glass of the globe. There was always kettles boiling on the kitchen range, and we had a primus stove, which heated water as well."*
Cynthia Worboys *(Oral History Recordings)*

The Recreation Ground

The village Recreation Ground of the 1940's was the original area of land purchased before the First World War. The Village Hall was built in 1927. During the war 'the rec.' was used for grazing cattle. VE celebrations took place on the 'rec.' and included a bonfire.

Games and sports, including football, cricket and tennis, were re-introduced after the war, although not on Sundays until 1959. The Parish Council agreed to ready the ground for football in 1947. The Tennis Club asked for permission to erect a fence around the tennis court in 1948 and in 1949 the Cricket Club asked for a concrete pitch for practice. The Recreation Ground was extended in 1991 by an additional 4.66 acres, doubling its size.

For extracts from the Village Hall minutes, see Chapter 9.

Transport

There were very few cars on the village roads in the 1940's. During the war of course there was petrol rationing and for some time no petrol was available except for official vehicles (which included farm vehicles).

People got around to a much greater extent than now on foot and by bicycle. All the children walked from home to the village school, with a round trip back for lunch. The American airmen based at Steeple Morden were issued with bicycles to get around the local area. There was the railway, with the station at Odsey, but comparatively few village people travelled on the train in the 1940's.

Taxis were used locally and there were services operated by Savages Garage in Hay Street, Steeple Morden and by Rules in Guilden Morden. Bus services for the village (operated by Eastern Counties) were more frequent than now and during the war men and women from the village took the bus to work in factories in Baldock and Letchworth.

"... it wasn't too bad (the bus service). *We were able to get into Royston, and we were able to get to Letchworth and Hitchin obviously because that's where we worked. The bus used to leave here at about eight in the morning and we used to get home round about half past six in the evening. Yes, that was quite good."*
Barbara Haines *(Oral History Recordings)*

Of course regular buses, lots of bus services, so you could get on a bus. Seven pence to go to Royston, twopence to go to Ashwell. Yeah, twopence to go to Ashwell to see my auntie. And that was when it was wet, if it was fine, then we could cycle, and save the twopence.

And it was seven pence to go to Royston, one and twopence return....."
Freda Adlington *(Oral History Recordings)*

The Police

The police officers stationed at Trap Road, Guilden Morden in the early 1940's were P.C. Venn followed by P.C. Cornwall.

"......Well the first winter we had to bike to Ashwell and be there at seven o'clock to catch the bus, and then when we come home we had to bike home, and it was a snowy winter. And the old coppers were always about, because you used to have a special rear light in them days, which you had a battery in. Well of course, if you turned it on and you got... we went over a bump that would perhaps shake it off. When I was working down there, at the beginning of the war, old Venn was copper about here, and I swear he always used to know what time I was... because I had to be in at ten, in the winter time I used to go back a bit earlier, and he would come creeping out from somewhere. 'Your rear light is not going again, I shall have to tell your father'. Well I said it was on when I started... I think he had me about three times [laughs].
Phyllis Dennis *(Oral History Recordings)*

"..... P.C. Venn, stationed at Guilden Morden, said in evidence, that at 10 p.m. on Dec 14th he kept observation on the appellant's premises. He saw several men leave just after 10 o'clock, but at 10.12 p.m. he could still hear voices in the taproom, and heard the front door locked on the inside. A little later, he heard the same voices coming from the living room..."
Report in the Royston Crow of February 1940 concerning Bertie Steel's appeal against conviction for supplying drink after hours in the Edward VII pub.

"..... P.C. Cornwall (Guilden Morden) said he was called to the accident at 7.50 a.m. The cycle was lying one foot from the left-hand wing of the car, and deceased was lying in the road three feet away from his cycle. He was bleeding freely from the head, and he also had a compound fracture of the right leg..... "
Report in the Royston Crow in December 1943 of the fatal death (sic) of Edward Thompson in an accident at the junction of Church Street and Trap Road.

Health and Welfare

Hospitals - Two hospitals were used locally during the 1940's; old Lister Hospital in Hitchin (replaced by the new Lister in Stevenage in 1972) and the old Addenbrookes in Trumpington Road, Cambridge (replaced by the new Addenbrookes at the end of Hills Road, Cambridge in 1976).

Ashwell Surgery

The local doctor's surgery was in Ashwell. Dr. John Moynihan took over the Ashwell Practice in 1934 and worked with his wife Dr. Sheila Moynihan. They had married in 1931. They moved the practice to *Stella House* in the High Street in 1952, eventually moving to *'The Avenels'* in Guilden Morden. Dr. Fergus Moynihan joined his father in 1965. Dr. Sheila had retired in 1948 and Dr. John carried on until his retirement on 31st December 1972 when he handed over to his son Fergus. The doctors both died in 1994, one year after their eldest son Peter, the actor famous for being the husband of 'Katie' of the Oxo advertisement.

ASHWELL,
BALDOCK,
HERTS.

JOHN H. MOYNIHAN, M.R.C.S., L.R.C.P.
SHEILA J. MOYNIHAN, M.R.C.S., L.R.C.P.

ASHWELL 30

1st July 1941

Mr Day

To
Dr. Moynihan
for Professional Attendance
to date.

£ 4 . 14 .

"..... The doctor we used to have to pay for, and I can remember my mum always had a glass on the sideboard for donations, that we always had to pay for the doctors. But we used to have... I think the doctor called more then.. now we have to go over to him....."
Cynthia Worboys (Oral History Recordings)

" ..... Talking about doctors and nurses etc., my mum's kitchen was the doctors surgery. He used to come Monday and Wednesday and Friday, that was Dr John Moynihan and he would come and patients who wished to see him would stand along the side of the house and wait for him to come. We never really knew what time he would come, but the days he was coming we had to get our breakfast done and get out of that kitchen so that it was ready for patients to come..... "
Barbara Haines (Oral History Recordings)

" ...... The Red Cross in Guilden Morden, there was no official men's Red Cross, it was all ladies. In fact I think they were quite impressive weren't they, I mean the ladies all... there were quite a lot of them, they were all quite efficient. They were all dressed immaculately in their photograph (see Chapter 11), and I was often erm... their guinea pig, because in those days Dr John, and Dr Sheila were the doctors around here, and the house we were talking about down the bottom of the lane – Bakers House – was empty, unused, and that turned into the Red Cross headquarters, the Red Cross/ARP headquarters. I can't remember which day it was, but I've got a feeling it was something like a Wednesday, every Wednesday

evening Dr John and Dr Sheila or one or the other would come and they would have the nurses all there, and they had to have patients with broken legs or broken arms and things like that, and that's what afflicted me for the rest of my life. I was always the one that had the broken leg and they would practice doing their bits and pieces...... Dr John and Dr Sheila lived in Ashwell, yes up the mount, opposite the springs, at the driveway right at the top there. When you went to the surgery you went up there, you couldn't bike up it, you had to walk up that bit, and then you parked your bike and you stood outside until they called you in, because there was only a little waiting room. You could only get about six in the waiting room. But they did a magnificent job really when you think of the area that Dr John... because Dr Sheila was always chief medical officer for Hertfordshire, I think, so she wasn't really in the Practice, she only helped out now and again. Dr John did it on his own. He had TB, he had lost a lung and he used to sleep in, what we would call a chicken house outside, because in those days that was the only cure. That sort of thing. Magnificent...."
John Dellar (Oral History Recordings)

".....Doctors, we used to go to Ashwell, had to go to Ashwell, and the doctor's surgery used to be up a steep hill, just nearly... past the recreation... opposite the Springs didn't it, you used to go to it, a drive way, that was just like a house. And the doctor used to come round if you was ill, he would visit. You always had visits from the doctor if you was ill. But you know, we weren't ill were we? We had chickenpox and little things children had, but we always went to school, we never got off school did we, when I think about it? No, no there was nothing, no what they call skiving today don't they? We daren't do that."
Freda Adlington (Oral History Recordings)

"..... I also have memories of our local doctor who was based in Ashwell and had Steeple and other villages. He had to come to me on several occasions, chickenpox, measles and whooping cough, so he must have had some difficult times, but life went on in spite of it all. When one recalls our quality of life it was pretty good, our childhood was not really spoilt, several restrictions but it became a way of life that we made the best of it..... "
Marjorie Baker (Memories of the War)

'The Felicity Mary Infant Welfare Clinic was started at the beginning of the Second World War, when many children were evacuated to Steeple Morden. The Red Cross team that was formed in the village was kept very busy caring for the young evacuees. Mrs Rigg, who lived at 'Orchards', Steeple Morden, provided a room at 'Two Trees' and money to equip the clinic. From these beginnings the present well-equipped Infant Welfare Clinic sprang. For a time it was held in a room at the 'One Bell', Steeple Morden; but after the building of Steeple Morden Village Hall in 1952 it moved into its own spacious quarters. Although it was 'taken over' at the coming of the Welfare State, the Clinic has retained its name and character, and is still run by a committee, who man its fortnightly sessions by rota. Doctor and nurse attend these sessions, and besides Guilden and Steeple Morden the clinic serves Litlington, Odsey and Croydon.'
Extract from the Womens' Institute Scrap Book of 1957. (The Clinic relocated to Guilden Morden Village Hall in 1949).

Interviewer

"You talk about Nurse Moss and Nurse Jarman, what did they used to do then?"

"Well obviously came round and... they came round and did a lot of visiting, all those people that needed help. And childbirth, they would have delivered the majority of the children, I suppose in those days. I don't think there was too many people that went to... had anything other than home births, I would remember. I think that at a young age we probably weren't allowed to know too much about that, to be honest, if I remember rightly"

Interviewer

"And of course they dealt with the nits as well, didn't they?"

"The nit... yes, they did, that's right. You regularly had the nit nurse come to school and look through your hair, yes. But I can't ever remember having nits, having them myself. Well nowadays I think they say you've got a clean head if you have them. In those days you'd got a dirty head."

Brenda Davies *(Oral History Recordings)*

Dentists

" .... from the school we used to have a mobile dentist come and he used to stand outside the vicarage on the wide path there and we used to go up from the school and get our teeth examined. Then if we had fillings to be done, or any extractions, they used to come back and do it.... "

Cynthia Worboys *(Oral History Recordings)*

"..... Royston, we had to go, or the school dentist, they used to come round. I used to have the school dentist, till I got a little bit older then I went to Royston, the dentist at Royston."

Freda Adlington *(Oral History Recordings)*

"..... Dentists: my first dentist that I recall was a Mr Boyd in Hitchin. And I can also tell you that he took... I can't remember much about my first two teeth coming out, but I can tell you that he came to Ashwell Road and removed eighteen of my teeth, along with Dr John. I can still remember this vividly and a nurse. I'm not sure whether it was Nurse Moss or Nurse Jarman, I can't remember which nurse.

But I had eighteen teeth out on the kitchen table. I can vividly remember that. And my aunt had this... probably an awful looking red handbag, which I very much liked as a child and actually when I came round she'd given me the red handbag with eighteen sixpences in. So, but could you imagine the dentist taking eighteen teeth out on the kitchen table today? In actual fact I did tell my husband's dentist that some years later and he looked at me horrified. He said, "We'd be struck off today if we were to do that". But I remember that very vividly".

Interviewer

"So you didn't use the dentist that visited the school then?"

"Yes, I did go to... I remember the school dentist. But I think my family chose to take me, if I needed anything done, take me to their own dentist......"
Interviewer
"In Hitchin?"
"Mhm."
Brenda Davies *(Oral History Recordings)*

".....We had a dentist come to the school, he used to come in a caravan and park outside the church on the large piece of pavement outside there. And he used to work the drill with his foot. He would stand there pressing this drill with his foot when he drilled your teeth and that wasn't just because it was a caravan. Because I went to a dentist in Letchworth after that and he was doing the same thing....."
Marie Parker *(Oral History Recordings)*

Chapter 6

Guilden Morden School

Education in Guilden Morden

Schoolmasters were recorded in 1582 and 1605. In 1599 a prosperous husbandman directed that his son be taught to read perfectly and write legibly. The parish had no school at around 1800, but by 1818 there was a Sunday school supported by subscriptions, with about one hundred pupils. In 1833 there were six day schools with forty four pupils paid for by their parents and two Sunday schools, one probably the church school, the other perhaps the origin of the British day school held by the Independents in their vestry c.1850. The church Sunday school was affiliated to the National Society by 1846, when it had about one hundred and forty pupils.

A National day school, then at the old vicarage, was moved by 1850 to a brick schoolroom and a teacher's house, built with the aid of a government building grant on a site given by Lord Hardwicke (see the extract from the Trust Deed at the end of the Chapter). Its thirty pupils were taught by a master and mistress, whose pay absorbed most of the £70 obtained from subscriptions and school pence[1]. In the 1860s that school had about one hundred pupils. The older children attended mainly in the winter, but few children in the parish were growing up entirely untaught.

The school was enlarged in 1867. The vicar also supported a night school from the 1840's to the 1870's. The proportion of the school's income raised from non-governmental sources fell from half of £170 in 1876 to only £60 of £270 by the late 1890's, when it was in financial difficulties. The average attendance was usually over one hundred and twenty before 1910. In 1885 there were seventy four older pupils and forty infants. Attendance declined from one hundred and nine in 1914 to sixty four by 1927 and forty seven by 1938.

From 1939 children from the Hungerford School in London were evacuated to Guilden Morden along with their Headmistress, Miss Still. From January 1940 they were taught separately in the Village Hall but in February 1942 they were absorbed into the village school.

The School Doctor, Dentist and Nurse examined the children regularly throughout the 1940's as there were frequent outbreaks of measles, chicken pox, mumps and influenza, as will be seen from the extracts from the school log.

From 1954 the older children went to Bassingbourn Village College. In 1972 some parents complained that the teaching was ineffective, only two pupils having

---

[1] In the late 19th and early 20th Century, parents had to pay a small amount each week for each child, to contribute towards the running costs of the school. This was originally 1d. Gordon Gentle was known to have recalled paying this.

passed the 'eleven plus' examination since 1965. In 1974 new school buildings were opened at Pound Green.[2]

Elizabeth Clark, a member of the chapel, kept a private school at Saville House from the 1890's to the 1920's.

Source: The Victoria County History of Cambridgeshire

1940 Infants

Top Row (left to right): Betty Evans, Marie Huffer, Jean Crow, John Bowen, Dennis Stephenson, Jack Waldock, Diana Tomlin. **Third Row:** Ron Clark, Jean Covington, Ann Merrill, Margaret Williams, Violet Peckett, Tate Twin Girls. **Teacher:** Miss Munden. **Second Row:** Marjorie Thompson, Brenda Thompson, Peter Turnell, Cynthia Peckett, Ruby Stephenson, Audrey Cheslyn, John Crow, James Crow. **Front Row:** John Dellar, Graham Dellar, Barbara Leonard, Freda Williams, Maureen Evans, Eileen Stephenson, Doreen Izzard, Victor Rose, Derek Dellar, Monica Flint.

1940 Juniors

Top Row (left to right): Rene Harding, Mary Perkiss, Brian Tomlin, John Jennings, Jessica Dellar, Mary Peckett. **Third Row:** Ron Bowen, Richard Murfitt, Doreen Pearce, Violet Horsley, Pearl Williams, Ronald Pameter, Miss Pullen (Headmistress). **Second Row:** Margaret Rose, Brenda Tomlin, Muriel Dellar, Fred Moule, Norman Williams, David Law, Elsie Tidy, Audrey Thompson, Jean Sole, Douglas Wiggett. **Front Row:** Betty Tidy, Jean Huffer, Maureen Carter, Joyce Law, Betty Peckett, Ken Williams, Megan Carter.

---

[2] See Appendix 4 for a photograph of the 'old school' in Church Street.

Extracts from the Head Teacher's Log in the 1940's
The Head had to record staff absence and some teachers were frequently affected by colds. The children recall the teachers always sitting near to the classroom stoves. Some children kept their coats on in cold weather.

January 11th 1940 - Furniture delivered so evacuated school (could be) moved to the Village Hall.
January 19th 1940 - The weather being very severe the temperature of the school has never been higher than 35 deg F this week. Attendance is exceptionally low.
January 29th 1940 - Heavy snowfall prevented some children from attending.
Feb 28th 1940 - Miss Pullen was absent suffering from laryngitis.
June 5th 1940 - Miss Pullen had the Managers' permission to attend the dentist this afternoon.
June 11th 1940 - Nurse visited and examined the children's hair.
Three tons of coal and 150 bundles of sticks delivered. These are emergency supplies.
June 20th 1940 - The dentist examined every child's teeth this morning.
July 12th 1940 - The school photographer came today.
September 16th 1940 - Nurse examined the hair of all children this morning.
September 17th 1940 - Air raid warning at 9.45am. Children dispersed.
October 7th 1940 - School roll now 55 resident children and 10 evacuees.
October 10th 1940 - An air raid warning was sounded at 3.15pm and the children dispersed immediately.
October 25th 1940, October 31st 1940, November 1st 1940 - Air raid warnings in the afternoon. Children dispersed. Notice was received that the dentist would visit the village in the clinic van to see the children whose parents have consented for them to be treated.
Nov 5th 1940 - The dentist brought the clinic van to the village. Some children will receive treatment tomorrow.
November 14th 1940 – Dr. John & Dr. Sheila Moynihan visited to inoculate the children whose parents had consented to their immunisation from diphtheria.
November 21st 1940 - The dentist visited and treated about another dozen children.
November 26th 1940 - Circulars about air-raid warnings and summer time received. The former cancels the plan to disperse the children when the alert is given. They are to go on with their lessons unless the parents request the child be allowed home. The government's decision to continue summertime has made it necessary to open school later. School will open at 9.30am, closing from 12.30pm until 1.45pm for lunch. Afternoon session will end at 4pm.
January 27th 1941 - Mrs. Munden was absent. Received a wire saying she was ill.
January 28th 1941 - Mrs. Munden returned to duty.
February 13th 194 - Mrs.Munden ill.
April 22nd 1941 - There was one case of measles reported.
April 30th 1941 - Acute shortage of coal. One ton delivered the following day.

May 19th 1941 - Miss Pullen went home at noon suffering from a cough and cold.

May 22nd 1941 - Nurse called to see a suspected case of scabies.

May 23rd 1941 - PC Venn called to enquire about bullets from a plane. He discovered several boys who had one or more and warned them it was an offence and also dangerous.

May 27th 1941 - Miss Pullen returned.

May 29th 1941 - Mrs. Munden had severe toothache necessitating immediate visit to the dentist.

June 12th 1941 - Nurse called for routine inspection and pronounced all the children clean.

June 30th 1941 - One case of chicken pox.

July 2nd 1941 - Several more cases of chicken pox.

July 13th 1941 - Only 30 children were present, the majority of absentees being excluded, suffering from chicken pox or contacts of those suffering.

July 15th 1941 - Notice of wartime holidays received. Children over 12 years may be absent from Sept 29th to Oct 11th for potato picking.

The headmistress married on December 31st and will continue in post as Mrs Kershaw.

January 12th 1942 - Demonstrators for the National Food Campaign called to arrange a demonstration of Wartime Cooking for Feb 6th in school.

January 28th 1942 - Notice from the Education Committee of amalgamation of the evacuated school with this on Monday February 2nd.

March 10th 1942 - Dr. Griffiths visited the school for a medical re-inspection.

May 4th 1942 - The school dentist visited for 3 days.

June 25th 1942 - Winter supply of coal delivered, six and a half tons.

July 13th 1942 - Dr. Brereton conducted a routine medical inspection.

September 7th 1942 - School opened with 58 local children and 13 evacuees.

September 22nd - Nurse made a routine inspection of the whole school.

October 19th 1942 - Mrs. Munden absent. She has undergone an operation for appendicitis.

November 16th 1942 - The Committee for Economy in Light and Heat recommended shorter school hours.

November 18th 1942 - Dr. Raven inoculated 20 children for immunization against diphtheria.

January 8th 1943 - One case of mumps and one of scabies reported.

January 13th 1943 - Nurse Moss called for hair inspection. Mrs.Jaquest absent suffering from a severe cold.

January 15th 1943 - Mrs. Jaquest returned.

January 21st 1943 - Dr. Brereton conducted a re-inspection this morning.

January 25th 1943 - Mrs. Munden went to consult a doctor in London.

May 21st 1943 - Dr. Brereton made a routine examination of the school children today. Nurse Moss was present.

May 24th 1943 - School reopened after Easter as a two teacher school, with 57 local children and 9 evacuees.

June 24th 1943 - The % attendance was below 60% owing to the measles epidemic.

July 5th 1943 - Mrs. Munden arrived at 11am having had a bilious attack.

July 21st 1943 - Dr. Brereton attended to examine all the children who had suffered from measles and whooping cough. Dr Raven called to give Dr Brereton the results and call his attention to particular cases.

September 21st 1943 - Nurse Moss made a routine inspection.

December 20th 1943 - Dr. Brereton visited and carried out the second medical examination of the year.

February 7th 1944 - The normal times of instruction were begun today. 9.00am to 12.00am and 1.30pm to 3.45pm.

February 22nd 1944 - The Speech Therapist called to advise regarding 3 children.

February 29th 1944 - The dentist arrived to examine and treat the children. Only 4 of those who needed treatment refused it. 25 children were treated. 18 were absent from school.

March 15th 1944 - School Nurse made routine inspection.

April 4th 1944 - Dr. Brereton made routine inspection of 26 children and re-inspected 12 others.

April 26th 1944 - Nurse Moss visited to examine and report on 4 special cases.

May 17th and 24th 1944 - Mrs. Kershaw visited the dentist

May 18th 1944 - Mr. W F Connor gave all the children 5/- (25p) each in 'Wings for Victory Week'. The money was paid into the School Bank.

May 25th 1944 - Mrs. Munden was ill and sent a telegram.

June 13th 1944 - Nurse Moss made the routine inspection.

July 18th 1944 - The village collected 4804 books for the national Book Recovery Drive.

September 12th 1944 - Mrs Kershaw began leave of absence while her husband was home on leave from the Royal Navy.

September 13th 1944 - Dr. Brereton visited for the re-inspection.

September 28th 1944 - Mrs. Kershaw had permission to close the Senior Class for several afternoons during her husband's leave.

October 9th 1944 - Infant Class closed owing to illness of Mrs. Munden. Severe cold and sore throat.

October 24th 1944 - A gift from Canada of sweetened chocolate powder has been given to provide a hot drink for the children who bring lunch for the break.

October 25th 1944 - Speech Therapist to arrange classes in Bassingbourn for child with a slight stammer.

November 13th 1944 - Mrs.Munden ill.

November 28th 1944 - Nurse Moss visited to see special cases.

December 5th 1944 - Dr. Brereton examined all the children today. She is conducting a nutrition survey.

December 6th 1944 - Mrs. Kershaw departed without notice. School closed for 3 days before supply arranged

January 30th 1945 - School closed because roads thick with snow.

May 1st 1945 - Miss S C Williams took charge. Dr. Brereton visited for routine medical inspection.

May 8th 1945 - Assembled for short service of Thanksgiving for Victory at 9am.

July 5th 1945 - School closed for General Election.

September 18th 1945 - Nurse visited for hair inspection.

November 6th 1945 - Nurse Moss called about two small children who needed attention.

February 11th 1946 - Nurse Moss visited; all clean.

March 8th 1946 - Speech Therapist saw 3 children.

May 13th 1946 - Nurse Moss gave head inspection.

May 23rd and June 24th 1946 - Visited by Henry Morris, Director of Education.

June 19th 1946 - London child could not attend secondary school interview owing to bad attack of mumps.

September 17th 1946 - Nurse Moss saw all children. All clean.

November 21st 1946 - Nurse called about 2 cases of whooping cough.

March 19th 1947 - Nurse gave child permission to return after complete recovery from scabies.

July 24th and 25th 1947 - Dentist visited.

Sept 16th 1947 - Nurse visited. Head inspection.

September 26th - 29th 1947 - School closed for Centenary Celebrations. The children received a New Testament and Psalms to mark the occasion.

November 19th 1947 - Nurse Moss inspected children – all clean.

November 20th 1947 - School closed for wedding of HRH Princess Elizabeth to Lt. Philip Mountbatten.

February 1948 - Senior boys are now attending Bassingbourn every Tuesday for Woodwork and Senior girls will attend Cookery and Handicraft.

April 19th 1948 - Dr. French M O visited to see deaf child.

June 3rd 1948 - Mr. Webster, Welfare and Attendance Officer called. Attendance very good.

July 19th 1948 - Miss O'Dell, Vice Principal of Wimpole Emergency Teacher Training College, enquired about students joining us for observation and teaching practice. Students will start on October 4th for 3 weeks.

October 21st 1948 - Mr. Wicksteed, a tutor at Wimpole Training College, gave a lecture on the course of the River Cam, he himself having sailed its course from Ashwell to Kings Lynn in order to film it.

February 3rd 1949 - Seniors and Juniors with Miss Coates (Student), came with me for a walk to Hooks Mill. Children found many specimens & signs of Spring & took particular notice of the River Cam. This Nature lesson lasted from 1.35 to 2.40.

April 6th 1949 - Miss Cade absent in the morning to attend a Managers' meeting at East Hatley in view of a Headship there. She was successful.

June & July 1949 - Miss Weatherly taught Hygiene to Seniors on Monday afternoons.

July 25th 1949 - Miss Weatherly showed a film to the Seniors, 'Healthy Living'.

July 29th 1949 - Miss Cade left today. We shall miss her very much.

September 13th 1949 - School re-opened today. Everywhere is newly painted, plenty of light and colour, certainly a wonderful improvement. Number on roll 48.

October 4th 1949 - School meals, served from Litlington Central Kitchen, began today.

October 6th 1949 - Miss I Hughes came to see the school before attending the Managers' meeting.

October 8th 1949 - Miss I Hughes accepted post of Headmistress of the school.

November 30th 1949 - Head teacher given send off with handsome clock & cheque on her retirement after four and a half years at Guilden Morden.

December 2nd 1949 - Miss I Hughes began duties as newly appointed Head Teacher of Guilden Morden School.

The Head Teachers during the 1940's were as follows:

1939-1944	Miss K M Pullen (Mrs. Kershaw)
1939-1946	Miss Still (Headmistress of the Evacuees)
1944-1945	Miss L Guffog (temporary)
1945	G E Wilkins
1945-1949	Miss S C Williams
1949-1958	Miss I Hughes

An Extract from the Trust Deed 1848
(Note the name of the witness at the end of document)

I CHARLES PHILIP YORKE Earl of Hardwicke of Wimpole Park in the County of Cambridge...DO hereby freely and voluntarily... grant and convey unto the Vicar and Churchwardens of the Parish of Guilden Morden ALL THOSE premises containing one rood and bounded on the North West by the Town street on the South East and South West by the Field belonging to me and on the North East by the Field belonging to Mary Ann Clark ... And upon trust to permit the said premises and all buildings thereon erected ... to be forever hereafter used as and for a School for the Education of Children and Adults of the Labouring Manufacturing and other classes...which said School shall always be in union with and conducted according to the principles ... of the National Society for promoting the education of the poor in the principles of the Established Church And further that the said School shall be open to the inspection of the Inspectors appointed... the Vicar shall have the superintendence of the moral and religious instruction of the Scholars ... the management direction control and government of the said School and of the funds... thereof and the selection appointment and dismissal of the Schoolmaster and Schoolmistress and their assistants shall be vested in and exercised by a Committee consisting of the Vicar and of six other persons of whom the following shall be the first appointed (namely) The Right Honourable the Earl of Hardwicke, The Master of Catherine Hall, Cambridge, Montford Strickland, Joseph Westrope, Frederick Butterfield and Richard Bowman all aforesaid Yeoman... being members of the Church of England......

IN WITNESS whereof the said Charles Philip Yorke Earl of Hardwicke hath hereunto affixed his hand and seal this 3rd day of October in the year of our Lord 1848..

Hardwicke

Robert Merry Vicar [of Guilden Morden]

SIGNED SEALED and DELIVERED... in the presence of B. Disraeli, M.P. for Bucks.

Chapter 7

Shops and Businesses

The Post Office and General Store
The owner of Guilden Morden Post Office and Store was A. E. Baker of High Street, Royston. The Shopkeeper and Postmaster was Mr. Day and later, Mr. Lavery. The Post Office Counter Clerk was Mrs. Marjorie Thompson and the Postman was her husband Mr. William Thompson. The Store was open Monday to Saturday with a half-day on Thursday.

The **Post Office** undertook many transactions such as pensions, savings, stamps, postal orders, wireless and dog licences as well as telegrams (few people had telephones) with messages written out and hand-delivered. The sorting office at Royston delivered mail daily to the Post Office for sorting and delivery by the village postman Mr. Thompson. He would collect mail from area postboxes at the end of each day to take to Ashwell Station on his bicycle for onward distribution via Cambridge.

The **General Store** had a main grocery area with a bacon slicer and cheeseboard. The main serving counter facing the door had brass scales with weights for weighing a variety of goods. Ledger books were ready for use and all around the walls were shelves with tinned goods, packets, bottles and jars containing jams and marmalades, with sauce bottles such as HP, Tomato Ketchup and Heinz Salad Cream. Different makes of tea such as Typhoo and Brooke Bond were sold and are still bought today. Biscuits and cakes, individual ones from Lyons like fruit pies, but others in slabs needing to be cut were available as well as fruit (oranges were a special treat during war years). Bread was baked at Lindsay's bakery. Bacon and cheese were kept in the cellar where it was cool, and the counter on which the bacon slicer and cheese board stood, with a wire to cut the cheese, was made of marble. These goods were cut and wrapped in greaseproof paper as were lard, butter and margarine. Sugar came in hessian sacks and was weighed in heavy-duty blue paper bags although some varieties of sugar were already in 2lb bags. Fresh milk was supplied by Murfitt's Dairy and there was also powdered milk and eggs. Fresh eggs came from a packing station in Royston near the Masonic Hall. Salt, gravy powder and pepper were weighed as required.

A small glass cabinet had sliding doors with medical items inside such as cough mixture, bandages, aspirin and embrocation for aching backs. Cigarettes and tobacco for pipe smokers were sold.

Washing powders such as Rinso, Oxydol and Lux Soap Flakes, and soaps for personal use with names like Lux, Palmolive and Lifebuoy, with Sunlight soap for household use, could all be bought. There was no soft toilet paper in those days but rolls of hard paper, and disinfectant called Izal ensured good hygiene in the home.

There was a small lending library in the shop. Haberdashery items of elastic, boot and shoe laces, and embroidery silks were sold and socks and other small items of clothing could be obtained. Stationery goods such as pens and pencils, crayons, ink, rubbers, sticky tape, balls of string for wrapping parcels to send through the post, could all be found.

Orders from shops outside the village e.g. Cambridge could be taken, as well as for items from pattern books such as wallpaper. Newspapers were delivered by Bert Steel, publican of the Edward VII and Mr. Dennis of Valley Farm.

As there was virtually no electricity in the village, oil stoves, lamps and candles were required for cooking, lighting and heating. Paraffin was a necessity and this was housed in a tank in a shed outside and customers would bring galvanised cans to be filled at 1/6d (7.5p) a gallon. Behind the shop were extensive gardens and an orchard where chickens were kept and fruit picked. Orders taken in the shop for home delivery were placed in what was called the 'trade bicycle' which had a carrier on the front in which to put a box or basket. On Saturdays a van from the Royston shop would deliver orders to outlying farms and areas.

"I just sat up in the corner of the Post Office .... (in a) high, very high chair and it had a rounded back, a wooden chair ... with a book or a pencil or some crayons or something and I had to sort of amuse myself. Well, I didn't have to spend too much time in the shop ... when my father was at home I was at home with him, and then I used to spend quite a lot of time with my grandfather who lived down New Road... but obviously at odd times I had to be in here or sitting waiting till mother had finished ... "
Marjorie Baker, daughter of William Thompson, village postman (Oral History Recordings)

William Thompson - Guilden Morden Postman
Mr. William Thompson, affectionately known as 'Bill', was the village postman for 47 years. He was a Guilden Morden man whose family were farm workers. His father worked at Rectory Farm for Mr. Hunt but he was apprenticed as a gardener to Morden House in Trap Road prior to serving in the First World War where he was wounded at the Battle of the Somme. On his return to Guilden Morden he became the Postman. The mail was delivered daily from Royston Sorting Office to local villages – each village had its own postman for sorting and delivery in their areas. Mr. Thompson had a Post Office bicycle to carry out his duties as postman. The mail arrived at the Post Office at 6 am for sorting and later delivery. From 3pm collections started with mail taken from the post box at Buxtons Lane to go to the Post Office where it was placed in a sack of mail from the Post Office box. Mail was then picked up from Steeple Morden Post Office and a post box in Litlington Road. Both sacks were then taken by Mr. Thompson on his bicycle to Ashwell Station to be sent to Cambridge by rail for onward delivery.

On Sundays, Mr. Thompson collected the mail from Guilden Morden, Steeple Morden, Litlington and Bassingbourn to take it to meet the Post Office van on the Old North Road in Kneesworth.

Mr. Thompson was entitled to two weeks holiday a year. His only day off was Boxing Day. On Christmas morning he delivered mail as usual. He worked until he was 70 years old as after this age he was entitled to an extra 5/- (25p) on the Post Office Pension. He died in 1975 at the age of 82 having served his village and surrounding area well.

Annie Murfitt's Shop

This 17th Century timber-framed house with outlying buildings was bought in 1918 by Miss Agnes Annie Murfitt to be used as her shop. In the 1940's it was a general store supplying dry goods, paraffin, sweets and milk from Murfitt's farm dairy. The store was taken over in 1946 by Sarah Stockwell (nee Watts) and her husband Samuel Charles Stockwell, the smallholder of Little Green Farm.

"The other shop I recall was one in the High Street near to Silver Street. It belonged to Miss Annie Murfitt, sister to Mr. Charles Murfitt, the farmer. This shop used to sell sweets and again goods of that nature and soft drinks. I do not know if any other goods were sold. My most vivid memory was going to the counter with my father to deliver the mail and if I were lucky he would buy me a quarter pound of sweets of my choosing. The sweets were displayed in big glass jars as one sees in pictures. Miss Murfitt was a plump elderly lady dressed in a black dress and apron and her hair was done in a bun and she wore glasses. The shop had a bell over the door and the entrance from the shop to the living quarters was a half glass and wooden door covered with net curtaining from which she would come when you entered the shop and the bell rang. She had a housekeeper Mrs. S Stockwell who you sometimes saw. Her husband had a smallholding down Little Green where his parents lived. His father had one leg and was a shoe mender by trade...."
Marjorie Baker (Oral History Recordings)

Lindsay's Bakery

George William Lindsay from Steeple Morden learned the bakery trade from Mr. Harper in Guilden Morden. In 1934 after working in London for a number of years he bought the bakery in Guilden Morden when Mr. Harper retired. At this time only about six people had cars in the village including the doctor and baker. In the 1940's electricity and a telephone were installed.

George Lindsay retired in 1947 when his son Sidney, who had been working with his father, took over the business. Although there was not a shop to buy goods, bread and other items could be purchased from inside the bakery. Bread was baked using flour provided by Cranfields of Colchester, and bakery sundries were supplied by the United Yeast Company (eg yeast and sugar). Orders were given one week for delivery the following week. Murfitt's dairy provided the milk. The bread was baked in two coke-fired ovens, one on top of the other, two more being added when electricity was installed giving four in total. There was a bread-cutting machine and a loaf of bread cost 4 $^1/_2$d (2p).

From 1948, after confectioner Frank Divinney was employed, sponges, fruit cakes, jam tarts, coconut pyramids, buns with butter cream topping, and so-called 'Eccles' cakes (using left-over currants/fruit from other goods) were made. Fancy cakes were sold - twelve to a box; and round meat pies with puff pastry and minced beef could also be bought. Bread could be bought at the bakery direct but Sidney Lindsay also had a bread round in Guilden Morden as well as to neighbouring villages. Eventually the bakery had several employees baking bread goods and confectionery, with four manning two delivery vans.

The business continued to expand but the bakery in Guilden Morden closed in 1971 following the death of Mr. Lindsay in a road accident. However, the family name continues as a bakery to this day, still serving fresh bread and cakes in shops at Potton and Bassingbourn..
Lindsay Bygraves, daughter of Mr Sidney Lindsay (Interview)

The Blacksmith
Next door to the Post Office and Shop Albert Kaye, then his son Oswald, had his forge where the farm horses were shod. Children at the school recall watching the horses standing patiently and remember the smell of hot iron when their shoes were being fitted.

The Cycle Shop
"Mr. Kaye the village blacksmith, who also ran a cycle repair and sales shop from his home on the corner of New Road also known as Kaye's Corner, did a roaring trade selling lamps and torch batteries. Talking of bicycles I can remember getting a new bike when the war was finished. It was a basic bike, no gears, called a Hercules. It cost £8 from there."
Marjorie Thompson (Oral History Recordings)

Shops delivering to Guilden Morden
International Stores delivered from Royston – orders taken one week and delivered the following week, as did the *Dunton Stores*. The *Co-operative Retail Stores (Co-op)* came to the village from Royston and goods could be bought from the van.

There were no butchers in Guilden Morden in the 1940's but neighbouring Ashwell had three. – *Crumps, Dennis's* and *Browns*. *Dennis's* and *Browns* closed in

1962 leaving *Crumps*. Mark Crump had taken over the business from the Flitton family in 1920 leaving it to his son Philip in 1954. Home deliveries were part of the service in the 1940's and orders placed on a Wednesday were delivered on the Saturday. The business is still family-run with Jonathan Crump now 'behind the counter' continuing to serve Ashwell and the surrounding area to this day but sadly no longer making home deliveries to Guilden Morden!

Coal Merchants *Thomas Moy*, and *Nash & Sons*, both from Royston, delivered coal and *Westropes* in Ashwell delivered paraffin and oil, as did *Fordham's of Odsey*.

Ironmongers *Halstead & Kestel* of Royston repaired agricultural equipment and made deliveries such as tin baths and other household goods. Biggleswade had a hardware shop which delivered goods.

   The landlord from the *'Pear Tree'* public house, James Wood, bought in vegetables to deliver round the area.

Tailor Although in the past there was a tailor in the village, the only service in the 1940's was a Mr. Armstrong from Duke Street, Bedford, who would call to take orders or measure one for perhaps a suit for later delivery.

Taxi Service A Vauxhall car was available as a taxi from Mr. Stanley Rule who had a smallholding in Dubbs Knoll Road. Prior to the 1940's his father had a bakery opposite the present school.

Garages There was no garage in Guilden Morden during the 1940's as there were virtually no privately owned vehicles until the late 1940's. *Savages Garage* in Steeple Morden ran a taxi service with Ford Pilot cars. They also sold accumulators for wirelesses and had on their premises the air-raid siren that was in use during the war.

Hairdressers and Barbers There were no hairdressers for women in Guilden Morden. Mr. Cyril Izzard of Avenel Terrace used to cut men's hair in his kitchen. His customers included the soldiers and German prisoners-of-war housed in the village. A barber, Simeon Starr lived in Swan Lane. He was a member of the Fire Service during the Second World War.

Builders and Undertakers John and Albert Worboys lived in Guilden Morden. John was both a builder and undertaker, building and repairing property and making coffins. Albert was the farmer.

   Aubrey Wright ran a funeral service from Steeple Morden.

Grave Diggers Several men in the village undertook the digging of graves for which payment was made by the Parish Council.

Chapter 8

Farming

Farming in the 1940's

1939 – 1945

Before the Second World War Britain imported fifty five million tons of food annually but by the end of 1939 this had dropped to twelve million tons. As a consequence, food rationing was introduced at the start of 1940 and did not completely end until July 1954. During this period there was a major effect on farming patterns – tractors slowly replaced horses but after the War the pace of change increased. Supplies, especially raw materials, were tightly controlled and resources were limited. The Government became involved with price fixing and subsidising to try and stabilise the fluctuating agricultural economy. As so many men were conscripted into the Armed Forces women were drafted in to work on the land. They were recruited by the Women's Land Army but popularly became known as 'land girls'. Older children were given time off school to help with jobs such as potato picking. Some of those from Guilden Morden are shown in the picture.

People were encouraged to grow their own food in Victory Gardens and householders to keep rabbits and chickens as well as growing vegetables.

Milk was a highly recommended food during the War as it was reasonably cheap and plentiful. From 1940 under the National Milk Scheme pregnant women and children less than five years old were issued with a pint of milk each day at a reduced price. For 'poor' families it was free. From 1941 eligibility was extended to new mothers, adolescents, invalids and institutions such as schools and hospitals.

1945 – 1949

The Agriculture Act of 1947 broadly revamped agricultural law. It aimed to safeguard food security so as to reduce the risk of a foreign power being able to starve the UK into submission. The Act guaranteed prices, markets and tenure so that a farmer could be assured his land would not be taken away and that crops would be sold at a known price. This was followed by the Agricultural Holdings Act of 1948 making it harder to evict tenant farmers. With the new security tenants enjoyed, a system of rent reviews became necessary to take account of land price inflation.

During the Second World War the National Farmers Union worked closely with the Ministry of Agriculture to ensure food security. Rationing continued after the War and it is a measure of the NFU's influence at that time that the Agriculture Act of 1947 committed the government to undertake a national review of the industry every year in consultation with the NFU.

National Farm Surveys of England and Wales 1940 – 1943

Due to the urgent need to increase food production the area of land under cultivation had to be increased significantly and quickly. County War Agricultural Executive Committees were established with powers to direct what was grown; to take possession of land; to terminate tenancies; to inspect property; and to organise mobile groups of farm workers.

One of the first responsibilities of the Committees was to direct a ploughing-up campaign under which large expanses of grassland were prepared for cultivation. Once the short-term objective of increasing food production had been met, thought was given to implementing a National Farm Survey with the longer-term purpose of providing data that would form the basis of post-war planning. Every farm and holding of five acres or more was to be surveyed.

A Primary Farm Record for each farm providing information on conditions of tenure and occupation; the natural state of the farm; including its fertility; the adequacy of its equipment and of its water and electricity supplies; the degree of

infestation with weeds or pests; and the management condition of the farm.

The complete 1941 census return for a farm including statistics of crop acreages and livestock numbers and information on rent and length of occupancy (see above and left).

A map of the farm was included showing its boundaries and the fields contained within it.

The National Farm Survey was begun in the spring of 1941 and largely completed by the end of 1943. Farms were visited and inspected, and farmers interviewed by District Committees.

Some 300,000 farms and other holdings were involved in the Survey. The cost was £20,000. A summary report was published in 1946.

Farms in Guilden Morden in the 1940's

The picture on the right shows Oswald Dellar on a traction engine at Rectory Farm.

The National Farm Surveys of England and Wales 1940-1943 included the following farms in the Guilden Morden area:

Cold Harbour Farm	S Kirby
Duck Lake Farm	J E and A F Worboys
Hooks Mill	E Carter
Home Farm	C Murfitt
Mobbs Hole Farm, Ashwell	C Murfitt
Morden Hall Farm	F H Kirby
Morden House Farm	D J Thompson
Rectory Farm	J W Smith & Son (Manager: Mr Jennings)
Town and Lodge Farms	W F Connor

These farms had livestock (cattle, dairy cows, pigs and poultry) and grew crops such as cereals, sugar beet, brassicas and potatoes. The village had a number of fruit orchards. There were also a considerable number of small-holdings tenanted by local families but owned by the then local authority as part of a First World War scheme. The picture shows Harry Dellar with a team of horses from Home Farm.

The Women's Land Army

Land girls from the Women's Land Army worked on some of the farms in Guilden Morden and nearby villages. One of these was Lily Willmott, who now lives in Steeple Morden with her husband Albert, who was born in this village. Some of her recorded memories are included below.

At the start of the Second World War when men were conscripted into the Armed Forces vacancies for working on the land were filled by women who had volunteered or been recruited to join the Women's Land Army. This was not a military force but uniforms were worn and the

For a healthy, happy job

Support the
WOMEN'S
LAND
ARMY
TRIBUTE

name of 'Land-girl' was generally used. Initially women had to be seventeen years old and attend a medical examination followed by an interview. They had to provide two character references and there was a check to ensure that they were not already in a reserved occupation. With the arrival of the National Service Act 1941 all women between the ages of twenty and thirty years were conscripted. This was later extended to nineteen to forty three years with appropriate exemptions. The choice was either working on the land or manufacturing.

Lily Willmott, applying with a friend to join up:
   "... so we went into town to join up and they said "how old are you?" "We said seventeen". "Oh no you can't ... the only thing you can do is go in the Women's Land Army."

In February 1943 there were fifty three thousand land-girls rising to sixty five thousand in June of the same year producing 70% of Britain's food. Recruitment stopped by decision of the War Cabinet in August 1943 as more workers were required for aircraft production but as of December 1943, eighty thousand land-girls were employed in agriculture. In January 1944 recruitment re-opened. Some of the land-girls received training before being sent to a farm but others were trained by farmers themselves 'on the job'.

Lily Willmott, on her training as a land girl:
   "Yes we went six weeks learning all about cows, breeds, diseases, how to look after them. That was at March in Cambridgeshire."

In August 1943 correspondence courses in agriculture and horticulture were introduced with Proficiency Tests. There was a wide range of jobs: milking cows, lambing, managing poultry, gathering crops, digging ditches, catching rats and farm maintenance according to the needs of the farm.

Lily Willmott, on her role as a land girl:
   "So we applied and I said ... anything, I will do anything in the Land Army, but I don't want to be with animals, so when my papers came through, I was a dairy maid! But I took to it, like a duck takes to water......went to Chatteris. It was a very...a very poor farm, sterilised all the milk in a copper, which you had to light a fire underneath. Milked the cows by hand and delivered the milk on a bicycle. People left the jugs out those days, with little bead covers on. You had two churns on your bicycle and you left the milk like that outside, wherever they had left their jug. There wasn't much hygiene there!"

After a short break, Lily returned to a farm in Steeple Morden – Morden Grange. This was a well equipped and modernised farm where she was happy to stay.

The land-girls came from a variety of backgrounds from cities and countryside. They wore a uniform of green v-necked jumpers, brown breeches or dungarees, brown felt hats, woollen socks and khaki overcoats with a badge depicting a wheatsheaf as a symbol of their agricultural work. (The picture shows Lily Willmott in the uniform). They earned the equivalent of £1.85 for a 50hr week increasing in 1944 to £2.85 but as individual farmers were responsible for payment it could not be guaranteed that these wages were in fact paid. Accommodation was on the farm itself or nearby, sometimes in hostels.

Lily Willmott on pay and conditions:
"Yes, (we were paid) 30 shillings (£1.50) and I used to send my mother 10 shillings (50p) home. I had a pound to last me all week. The Land Army paid 30 shillings for our board and lodgings. We were billeted at the schoolhouse in Odsey.

Well, we got half a day a week off I think, because we had to go in Christmas Day and New Years Day, Sundays ....well every day, the cows had to be milked twice a day. We used to get leave...we used to get about a week's leave, I think it was after three or four months, something like that."

There was an official Women's Land Army magazine and the land-girls had a special song:
'Back to the land, we must all lend a hand
To the farm and the fields we must go
There's a job to be done
Though we can't fire a gun
We can still do our bit with the hoe'

In 1942 the Timber Corps was introduced when six thousand Lumber Jills were recruited. This Corps was a separate branch of the Women's Land Army and was formed because of a shortage of imported wood used not only in agriculture but also for making wooden props in mines.

The Women's Land Army was disbanded in 1950. Many of the Land-girls and Lumber Jills made friendships which lasted throughout their lives.

Chapter 9

Sport and Leisure

In the 1940's, as now, many social and sporting activities took place in the setting of the Village Hall and Recreation Ground. The Village Hall was built in 1927. During the 1940's, it was used extensively for dances, whist drives, meetings and 'socials'.

Extracts from the minutes of the Village Hall Management Committee:

1940 - The Village Hall is to be used as a school for evacuated children. The Village Hall to be used as a shelter for people made homeless as a result of air raids. The County Council would provide the necessary equipment and pay expenses for lighting and heating. Miss Still, the Headmistress of the Hungerford Road School (the evacuees), asked permission to install a wireless set for school use. The Home Guard is to use the hall once a week.

1943 - Christmas money should be put by for the three prisoners of war. A Whist drive and Dance held for the 'Aid to Russia Fund'. The Parish Council gave permission for a coal shed at the end of the Hall. New blackout needed. Carried unanimously that water be brought in to the Recreation Ground and laid on in the Village Hall kitchen.

1944 - It was agreed that a placard be put up prohibiting alcoholic drinks from being brought in. It was agreed by the committee that the Italians were not to be allowed into the Dances.

1945 - A new lock was needed for the lavatory, also a pail, shovel and rake. Two of the Hall windows found broken after VJ night.

1946 - Dancing classes were arranged (lower age limit 14 years). A raffle was suggested; Mr. Lindsay promised an iced cake; Mr. Dellar a fowl; and Mr. Gentle a rabbit.

1947 - A Beetle Drive was held. New records were needed for Old Time and Modern Dances. The Sports and Fete Committee offered the proceeds of the Fete to the Village Hall Committee towards building a kitchen and cloakroom on the Hall (£50).

1949 - Plans discussed for an additional building – kitchen, coal store and lavatory. Felicity Mary infant welfare centre to move to the Village Hall. A licence was required to hold a pantomime.

The Recreation Ground of the 1940's was the original area of land purchased before the First World War. During the war 'the rec.' was used for grazing cattle. VE celebrations took place on the 'rec.' and included a bonfire. Games and sports, including football, cricket and tennis were re-introduced after the war, although not on Sundays, until 1959. The Parish Council agreed to ready the ground for football in 1947. The Tennis Club asked for permission to erect a fence around the tennis court in 1948, and in 1949 the Cricket Club asked for a concrete pitch for practice.

The Women's Institute

The aim of the WI Movement was to 'Improve and Develop Conditions of Rural Life'. The Women's Institute (formed here in February 1933) held monthly meetings alternately in Guilden and Steeple Morden. These took place in the afternoon during winter and evenings in the summer. They were held at various venues during the 1940's usually the Methodist School Room in Steeple Morden and the Village Hall or Congregational Schoolroom in Guilden Morden. The WI had an annually elected President, Secretary, Treasurer and Committee, voted by members. For most of the 1940's, Mrs. Bayne-Jardine of Riversdale was the President and Mrs. Doris Jarman was Secretary. Membership varied from thirty seven to fifty with average attendances of fifteen to twenty. This was believed to be because members were from two villages and transport was usually on foot or by bicycle. The monthly meetings would have a speaker and topics were very varied. Examples such as The Difficulties of the Blackout, Growing Vegetables, Care of the Feet, Make Do and Mend, Work of the Parish and District Council, The Value of the Empire, The Changing Face of Europe, Music of Handel, A Woman Magistrate, My Duties as a District Nurse and String Bags and Belts. Sometimes there would be demonstrations e.g. War-time Cookery, Using Potatoes and How to Pulp and Bottle Fruit. A Ministry slogan at the time was 'Bread Costs Ships, Eat Home Grown Potatoes Instead'.

Activities during the war years

Working parties instigated by Mrs. Bayne-Jardine (WI President) and directed by the Wool Dept. of Cambridge WVS were formed in various member's and non-member's homes in both villages to knit items for Cambridgeshire men on active service. The Girl Guides organised a weekly collection of paper which was sold to raise money for the purchase of wool. The last meeting was held on 20th Jan.1945 and the knitters, not all WI members, were congratulated by Mrs. Ransome of the WVS on the quality of the knitting, stating that it was the best in the county. Some of the participants were Mrs. Worboys who knitted two hundred and twenty eight items, Mrs. Conder one hundred and seventy eight items and Mrs. Turnell one hundred and fifty three items. Garments were also knitted for the evacuees. The WI President organised the collection of scrap metal for the war effort. Dumps were set up in both villages. In 1940, 859lbs of plum jam was made at *'Riversdale'* (the WI President's home) and soon sold in aid of National Service Activities.

Onion, tomato and vegetable seeds received from the Canadian Federation of WI's were distributed in both villages. The WI was involved in the 'Penny-a-week' collections for the Red Cross Agricultural Fund.[1]

Eggs were collected for Royston Hospital, books collected for the Merchant Navy, warm clothing collected for women and children in Soviet Russia, toys collected for an evacuated nursery school and generous collections of onions sent to a WI in Bishop Auckland. A Christmas Party for members and the elderly in both villages was organised each winter with over ninety people attending. In August 1944 the WI organised the Flower and Produce show in Guilden Morden.

The WI still exists today, meeting on the 3rd Thursday of each month in Guilden Morden Village Hall. It is now known as 'The Mordens WI'.

Guides and Brownies

There was no Scout Troup in the village but there were Guides and Brownies.

"I did join the Girl Guides. I wasn't in the Girl Guides for very long, maybe a year or so. But one of the very funny things, when I was there I got a badge for needlework, and I am the most... well, I just got no idea of needlework, and my father always says to me, "You've got the badge to show it", and I have, I do know where that badge is today. Miss Price used to do the Guides. We used to go to the vicarage. Quite often it was in the garden, when it was a decent day, and we did do various things. But I got very fed up with that, so I gave that up."

Marie Parker (*Oral History Recordings*)

Back Row (left to right): Betty Platt, Jean Crow, Violet Peckett, Margaret Williams.
Front Row: Betty Evans, Ann Barratt, Miss Price, Dorothy Mence, Jean Covington.

Back Row (left to right): Muriel Kirbyshire, Sylvia Gentle, Jean Mence, Freda Williams, Miss Price, Cynthia Peckett, Mary Williams, Barbara Leonard, Iris Gentle. Sitting: Sheila Williams, Lindy Lindsay.

"We had the Brownies in the vicarage. Well I remember we had Brown Owl....We always played games and she took us for walks. We used to have like a bonfire...well it wasn't a bonfire it was a log of wood, and we used to grate up candle and we had candle wax and sawdust, and burnt it on the log of wood, and we sang our songs around it.

Cynthia Worboys (*Oral History Recordings*)

---

[1] *The Red Cross Agricultural Fund – launched in September 1939 by the Duke of Gloucester and known as the Red Cross & St John Appeal Fund to raise funds for those affected by the Second World War.*

Football

As the Recreation Ground was unavailable, there was very little organised sport in Guilden Morden during the war. However, from the 1947/48 season things returned to normal. The picture below shows one of the first post-war Guilden Morden football teams.

Back Row (left to right): Derek Moore, Richard Murfitt, Arthur Henman, Les Huffer (standing in for Brian Tomlin), Harry Hart, Ernie Dore. **Front Row:** *Alf Mynott, Fred Kirbyshire, Sid Thompson, Lou Barratt, Jack Dellar.*

The following picture shows a young football team from the late 40's/early 50's.

Left to Right: John Dellar, John Peckett, Ron Dellar, Bernard Gray, Derek Dellar, Bryan Dellar, Peter Turnell, Pete Dellar, Jamie Crow, Graham Dellar, Tony Williams.

Pubs

There were six licensed premises in the village during the 1940's[2]. There were two categories of license at this time – a Beer House license which allowed the licensee to sell beer and cider and a Full License which also allowed the sale of wines and spirits. Beer Houses were often family homes using a room or cellar to store the barrels of beer and another room in which to sit and drink it. Beer was either home-made or supplied by a brewer.

The Beer Houses in Guilden Morden were:

The Black Horse on Potton Road (ceased trading 1956)
Owner: Wells & Winch Ltd   Landlord: Frank Bonfield
The Chestnut Tree in the High Street (ceased trading 1959)
Owner: E.K. &H. Fordham   Landlord: George Charles Reynolds
The Edward VII on Fox Hill Road
Owner: E.K. &H. Fordham   Landlord: Bert Steel
The Pear Tree, Great Green (ceased trading 1960)
Owner: Wells & Winch Ltd   Landlords: Walter Covington, James Woods

---

[2] Photos of all these premises are shown in Appendix 4.

The Full License premises were:

The Six Bells Fox Hill Road (ceased trading 1963)

Owner: Wells & Winch Ltd   Landlords: Frank Hayward, Alfred William Essam, William Henry Brooks, Arthur Sidney Brooks, Frederick William Blake

Three Tuns (Full License from 1948) in the High Street (ceased trading 2013)

Owner: Wells & Winch Ltd   Landlords: William Richard Cheslyn, Emily Elizabeth Cheslyn, John Gray, Emily Cheslyn, Arthur Claude Pearce

Local Breweries

Biggleswade Brewery - There was a brewery site in Biggleswade in 1686. In 1794 Samuel Wells of Baldock purchased the brew house. He died in 1831 and the business passed to his two sons-in-law when it was renamed Wells and Company. In 1898 the brewery was put up for sale. George Winch of Chatham, Kent bought it for his son Edmund and in 1899 it became known as Wells & Winch Ltd. The company was at its peak in 1938 with three hundred and eighty three public houses and was still expanding the Biggleswade site but between 1939 and 1945 it had to accommodate a number of restrictions leading to it becoming the sole local supplier of soft drinks. Wells & Winch Ltd of Biggleswade was sold to Greene King Ltd in 1961 changing its name in April 1963. It closed in 1997.

Fordhams Brewery - In 1796 E.P. Fordham of Ashwell took over the lease of land in Ashwell from the Whitbread family in order to establish a brewery. By 1864 they traded as E.K. & H. Fordham with a considerable property portfolio and in 1897 it was registered as a limited company. It was acquired in 1952 by J.W. Greene Ltd of Luton but ceased to brew beer and became a bottle store before closing in 1965.

Simpsons Brewery - In 1855 Simpsons Brewery of Baldock bought the 'Three Tuns' in Guilden Morden and licensed it as a Beer House with tenants until 1948 when it became fully licensed. In 1954, when Wells & Winch then owned it, it was sold to Greene King Ltd.

The Wireless

"The radio was a source of information about the theatres of war, but it was operated by an accumulator which was replenished by Messrs Pepper and Haywood in Royston every fortnight. Shows like ITMA, Family Favourites and Children's Hour I was allowed to listen to. The accumulator often ran down before two weeks so had to be boosted by a two cell cycle lamp battery, then it was news only. The daily service and the six o'clock news were most listened to I think. The King's Christmas speech was also important. I never got to listen a lot in the evenings as homework and piano practice was the priority".
Marjorie Baker *(Memories of the War)*

The Balalaika Players

The photograph shows some of the boys who played in the band. **Back Row** *(left to right): Ronald Dellar (Guilden Morden), Eddie Lucas, Tommy Turnham (Steeple Morden), Graham Jarman (Steeple Morden) Bryan Dellar (Guilden Morden).* **Front Row** *(left to right): Brian Melody (Litlington), Terry Bird (Litlington), Robert Birse, Graham Dellar (Guilden Morden), Alastair Mountain (Litlington).*

'The balalaika is well known as the traditional Russian instrument and it is therefore a little surprising to find a group of exponents of the instrument tucked away in rural Hertfordshire. Upon investigation the reason is at once apparent, for the village of Litlington (nr. Royston) is the home of R.A. Birse and the rest of the combination are all his pupils. We have become so used to the general scramble for the limited number of players that it is indeed refreshing to find a teacher like R.A.Birse who can first stimulate local interest and ultimately create a charming and efficient combination like the 'Balalaika Players'. The combination was started in 1947 by R.A.Birse with the assistance of his pupil Joe Buchan. 'Bob' Birse learnt to play the balalaika when a boy in St Petersburg. His tutor was Henry P. Sanders the right hand man of V. Andreyeff. Henry P. Sanders is the father of the film star George Sanders. He is now 84 years of age but in March 1951 he travelled from Surrey to London to hear the 'Balalaika Players' perform.

Joe Buchan, just out of his teens has acquired an excellent technique under the schooling of Mr Birse. In 1950 he was the winner of the Birse/Perott Cup at the Federation Festival. Joe is at present absent from the group as he is on service in Korea.

The group started modestly enough making appearances in village halls but later graduated to the Town Hall at Royston and ultimately television and radio. They have made several performances before H.H. Princess Marie Louise and now possess the honour of her patronage. On a recent appearance H.H. Princess Marie Louise congratulated the boys upon the interesting hobby they had taken up.'

The above article appeared in Bulletin No.6 of The British Federation of Banjoists, Mandolinists and Guitarists (Southern Section) in February 1952.

The following articles appeared in the Royston Crow. We are indebted to the Royston Museum for allowing us to research their copies of the Royston Crow for these articles.

R.A.F.A.'s Talent Competition, 16th September 1949

'A special prize was awarded to Mr. Birse and his Balalaika Band. Prior to the war, Mr. Birse himself trained a number of boys to play this early Russian instrument, of which he possesses 22, but the war made disbandment a necessity. Now, having started again from scratch, Mr. Birse has formed a pleasing little combination of five players.'

Abington Pigotts, 14th October 1949

'The Balalaika Concert Party gave a concert at the Village Hall at Abington Pigotts on October 14th, in aid of the Litlington Church Restoration Fund. The Balalaika Players led off with some of their popular tunes. Joe Buchan's balalaika solo held out great promise of his becoming an expert player. There were two sketches given by the boys, and the pleasing playing of the Balalaika Orchestra ended quite an enjoyable evening.'

Concert at Bassingbourn County School, 11th November 1949

'Mr R.A. Birse and his Balalaika Boys were responsible for the very charming entertainment given in the School, Bassingbourn, on Friday last, 11th November. Russian costume and tunes had the authentic tone, and the band have developed considerably since its performance in the Pantomime last year. The two songs sung with the orchestra by the compère, Mr. Roy Oxenford, had something of the real abandon of those exciting Russian folk tunes.'

Picture Page
(The Balalaika Players made their first and only TV appearance on 'Picture Page' in 16th November 1949)

'The television sets around Royston, Litlington and the Mordens were working overtime and to 'crowded audiences' on Wednesday of last week, when the Balalaika Players, under their director, Mr. Birse, appeared on 'Picture Page.' The orchestra was composed of Joe Buchan, Cyril Bird, Tommy Turnham, Eddie Lucas, Kenneth Jarman, Gerald Sale and Graham Dellar. They were auditioned in Mr. Birse's studio in Litlington, and on Wednesday evening were taken to Alexandra Palace in a B.B.C. coach, where the boys were shown the inner workings of a television studio.

Their performance took place at 10 p.m. and as a result, the Players received an invitation, written that same evening, to give a concert in the Cambs. district.

Joan Gilbert, the television announcer, has written to say that she hoped the boys enjoyed their visit. She thought them "awfully good," and continued, "I hope you will tell them on my behalf how much pleasure they gave us.

Many letters of congratulation have been received, and a representative of a National Weekly came down on Monday to interview them.'

Concert at Ashwell, 10th December 1949

'The Variety of the Concert, held in the Congregational Schoolroom, and organised by the members for church funds was greatly appreciated by a good audience, who packed the building on Saturday last, December 10th. In the concert, were featured the Litlington 'Balalaika Boys Orchestra,' under their leader and teacher Mr. Birse. The whole show was introduced by Mr. Oxenford as compère, who also rendered humorous songs accompanied by the Balalaikas.'

The following is a list of appearances by the Balalaika Players in the 1940's:

2nd Nov 1947	Recital to parents in R.A.Birse's music room.
6th Dec 1947	Recital to Mrs. Stokes in the music room.
19th Dec 1947	The Shrubbery School at Cambridge.
16th April 1948	For the Conservative Association at the Bull Hotel, Royston.
12th May 1948	The Cambridgeshire County High School for Girls.
14th May 1948	The Alliance Hall, Baldock.
17th May 1948	Litlington Vicarage.
25th May 1948	Bassingbourn County School.
20th June 1948	For the Royal Air Force at Bassingbourn.
13-15th Dec 1948	In the Bassingbourn County School Pantomime.
1st March 1949	For the Boy Scouts, Royston.
18th March 1949	The Alliance Hall, Baldock.
18th April 1949	Steeple Morden.
20th April 1949	At Mrs. Jenner's Party at the Bull Hotel, Royston.
22nd April 1949	For the Conservative Association at the Bull Hotel, Royston.
25th April 1949	St Neots.
13th May 1949	At a Grand Concert at Abington Pigotts Village Hall.
26th May 1949	Litlington Youth Club.
6th June 1949	Steeple Morden.
13th June 1949	For the RBL (Womens' Section) at the home of Mrs. E. Pepper.
21st July 1949	Ashwell Womens Institute.
29th July 1949	At a Concert Party, Guilden Morden.
16th Sep 1949	At an R.A.F.A. Talent Competition, Royston Town Hall.
14th Oct 1949	At a Concert at Abington Pigotts Village Hall in aid of Litlington Church Restoration.
5th Nov 1949	Television audition at Litlington.
11th Nov 1949	At a Concert at Bassingbourn County School.
16th Nov 1949	Appearance on BBC TVs *'Picture Page'* at Alexandra Palace, presented by Joan Gilbert.
10th Dec 1949	At a Concert at Ashwell Congregational Hall.
17th Dec 1949	The Atlas Stone Works, Melbourn.
22nd Dec 1949	For the Royal Air Force at Bassingbourn.

The players went on to crown a wonderful career by appearing before the Queen and Prince Philip at Luton Hoo on 23rd November 1952.

Chapter 10

Wartime Conditions

The Blackout

The blackout was imposed on 1st September 1939, in the belief that this would make it difficult for the Luftwaffe to navigate and find targets. The ban was total – no chinks of light through curtains; no streetlights; no car headlights. The government ensured that sufficient blackout material was available for all households. Putting up the blackout material was an arduous task, ensuring that no light could be seen from outside. The ARP wardens could report householders who did not follow the rules and fines or court appearances often resulted. The blackout rules were a significant task for factories, particularly if they had glass roofs. Shopkeepers were also affected.

On the roads there was a significant increase in accidents. The introduction of white lines down the centre of roads and painting kerbs white helped to some extent. Speed limits were reduced from 30 mph to 20 mph.

There was some increase in the level of crime, although not as much as had been feared. Torches could be used but had to be pointed downwards. From September 1944 the restrictions were relaxed. Street lighting returned in April 1945. Symbolically, Big Ben was illuminated again on 30 April 1945.

"Earliest events were to do with the taping of the windows, an X on every pane. This was to prevent the glass shattering. Next item was the blackout blinds and curtains. No lights must be seen. Every window must be done. Air Raid Wardens used to patrol at night and if you had a light showing you were reprimanded, the reason being enemy aircraft would be able to see where you were. No visible lights were allowed. I remember the village hall had big blackout curtains. It was coarse plain material, no patterns of course.... bicycle lights had to be dimmed. A piece of greaseproof paper was used to dim the front light, and a piece of red paper the back. The buses were equipped with blackout curtains and had a substance to seal the windows against shattering."
Marjorie Baker (Memories of the War)

Air Raid Shelters

Some people made their own shelters but 'Anderson Shelters' were available made of galvanised corrugated steel. These were free to families earning less than £250 p.a.. There were also 'Morrison Shelters' which were like a reinforced metal dining room table.

".... in the garden we had an air raid shelter built of sacks and sand and a part brick concrete floor, galvanised tin roof, but we never used it. My Dad stored his potatoes in it..... Also I remember being told that there was one in the field next to the shop (i.e. the Village Post Office) for public use. I never went in it. This was before the bungalow was built and it used to be a cabbage field."
Marjorie Baker (Memories of the War)

"During the war our dugout was in the field next to our garden, that is now Bells Meadow. I can remember going down there when the siren went. I had a lovely black eiderdown with red roses on it and I always took it with me."
Barbara Haines (*Memories of the* War)

Identity Cards

In the UK we have a census every ten years (e.g. 1911, 1921, 1931, etc.). For 1941, however, there was no census – instead we had 'National Registration'. The National Registration Act of 1939 established a National Register which began operating on 29 September 1939 (National Registration Day). A system of identity cards was introduced. These had to be produced on demand or at a police station within forty eight hours. The system was introduced as an instant census, to be used for rationing, planning decisions and manpower control to maximise the efficiency of the war effort.

The identity cards had the following codes:

A - for those aged over twenty one.

B - for those aged between sixteen and twenty one.

C - for workers from the Irish Republic (yellow cards).

N - for cards re-issued under an altered name.

V - for those aged over sixteen who declared they were usually resident outside the UK.

The requirement to carry an identity card ceased in February 1952.

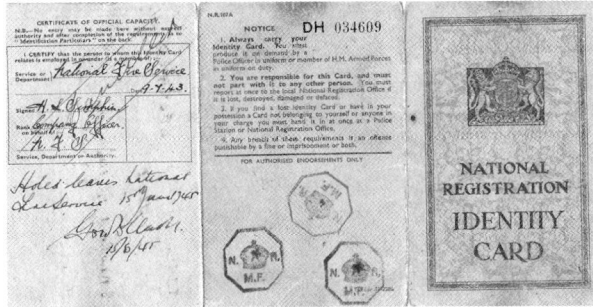

Gas Masks

It was feared that the population in the UK would be subject to gas attacks, following the experience in the First World War when gas was used extensively on the Western Front. Also gas had been dropped by bombers during the Spanish Civil War.

By September 1939, some thirty eight million gas masks had been handed out to households. It was the responsibility of the ARP wardens to ensure that all civilians had a gas mask. They were never needed.

"Now the next most important item was the gas mask. Everyone was issued with one. It consisted of a cardboard box with a handle of string threaded through to carry on your shoulder or back. The box got damaged and had to be stuck up with tape. You took it everywhere you went out. My father had one in a metal container. Being a postman this was to protect it from the elements. I still have it today. Going to school as I did on a bus, a satchel plus a gas mask was quite hard work!"
Marjorie Baker (*Memories of the* War)

Rationing

Rationing was necessary mainly because of the reduction in imports due to enemy action against shipping during the war and also the diversion of resources to meet wartime production for military purposes. One month after the war started imports of food were down to twelve million tons p.a. compared to fifty five million tons before the war. Rationing lasted from January 1940 to July 1954 – fourteen years. The 'Dig for Victory' campaign encouraged people to dig up their gardens and grow food.

Food

Ration books were issued for every person. You had to register with the shops that you wanted to use. Items were crossed off by the shopkeeper as purchases were made. Rationing of food started at different dates, e.g.

Jan 1940	Bacon, butter and sugar
Mar 1940	Meat (rabbit and pigeon were not rationed)
Jul 1940	Cooking fat, tea
Mar 1941	Jam
May 1941	Cheese
Jun 1941	Eggs
Jan 1942	Rice, dried fruit

Due to the harsh winter of 1946/47, frost destroyed a huge amount of stored potatoes – potato rationing started.

"...We used to eek out our rations of course, and you would swop things with people ...say for instance somebody in Steeple Morden didn't like cheese, so we used to swap some sugar with their cheese ration, things like that. I used to have to walk across the fields from Guilden Morden to Steeple Morden to deliver this stuff and bring the cheese back."
Graham Dellar *(Oral History Recordings)*

"...and I do remember that they came up with a mixture of cornflower and egg which they mixed with real butter to make it go further. It was like, almost a spread than a butter, but it did eek things out."
John Dellar *(Oral History Recordings)*

"...and there used to be some sort of fish come, South African fish[1]. It began with a "s" I think, but it was some sort of substitute it became popular as a substitute for other things that we couldn't get, you know."
Marjorie Baker *(Oral History Recordings)*

---

[1] The fish was snoek, a type of mackerel. Fish wasn't rationed but was expensive due to the reduction in fishing activity.

Rations varied but a typical ration for one adult per week would be:

    Butter 2oz
    Margarine 4oz
    Bacon & ham 4oz
    Sugar 8oz
    Tea 2oz
    Milk 3pints
    Meat to the value of 1/2d (about 6p)
    Cheese 2oz
    Eggs 1per week (vegetarians were allowed 2)
    Dried eggs 1 packet every 4 weeks
    Jam 1lb every 2 months

There was also an allowance based on points for tinned and dried food. Meat rationing continued until June 1954.

The National Loaf

This was made of wholemeal bread and an order was made that it could not be sold until the day after it was baked. This was because it is easier to slice it thinly when it was not fresh and also because people would eat more if it was freshly baked.

In 1946 bread too was rationed. Continual rain had ruined the wheat harvest in that year.

Confectionery

Confectionery rationing ended in February 1953.

"The best part was the sweet ration, each month my mother went to Hitchin or Letchworth shopping. It was half day at the village shop and post office. We used to go to a sweet shop in Hitchin churchyard called Garrat & Cannons. They were sweet manufacturers. The sweets stood on shelves in big jars all labelled. One was allocated 1lb of sweets per month. My dad always had extra strong peppermints and my mother barley sugar. I had all kinds".
Marjorie Baker (*Memories of the War*)

Clothes

Clothes rationing was introduced in the summer of 1941 with an annual ration of 66 coupons.

This was based on the provision of a complete set of clothes for each person per year. People were urged to 'Make do and mend'. Every item of clothing had a value in coupons – see following lists.

Women and Girls	Adult	Child
Lined mackintoshes, or coats (over 28in. Long)	14	11
Jacket, or short coat (under 28in. in length)	11	8
Dress, or gown, or frock - woollen	11	8

Women and Girls (cont'd)	Adult	Child
Dress, or gown, or frock - other material	7	5
Gym tunic or girl's skirt with bodice	8	6
Blouse, or sports shirt, or cardigan, or jumper	5	3
Skirt, or divided skirt	7	5
Overalls, or dungarees, or like garment	6	4
Apron, or pinafore	3	2
Pyjamas	8	6
Nightdress	6	5
Petticoat, or slip, or combination, or camiknickers	4	3
Other undergarments, including corsets	3	2
Pair of stockings	2	1
Pair of socks (ankle length)	1	1
Collar, or tie, or pair of cuffs	1	1
Two handkerchiefs	1	1
Scarf, or pair of gloves or mittens, or muff	2	2
Pair of slippers, boots, or shoes	5	3

Men and Boys	Adult	Child
Unlined mackintosh or cape	9	7
Other mackintoshes, or raincoat, or overcoat	16	11
Coat, or jacket, or blazer or like garment	13	8
Waistcoat, or pullover, or cardigan, or jersey	5	3
Trousers (other than fustian or corduroy)	8	6
Fustian or corduroy trousers	5	5
Shorts	5	3
Overalls, or dungarees or like garment	6	4
Dressing-gown or bathing gown	8	6
Night-shirt or pair of pyjamas	8	6
Shirt, or combinations - woollen	8	6
Shirt, or combinations - other material	5	4
Pants, or vest, or bathing costume, or child's blouse	4	2
Pair of socks or stockings	3	1
Collar, or tie, or pair of cuffs	1	1
Two handkerchiefs	1	1
Scarf, or pair of gloves or mittens	2	2
Pair of slippers or goloshes	4	2
Pair of boots or shoes	7	3
Pair of leggings, garters or spats	3	2

Coupons were printed in different colours and the government announced when each colour could be used. Clothing 'points' were gradually reduced during the war. Clothes rationing ended in March 1949.

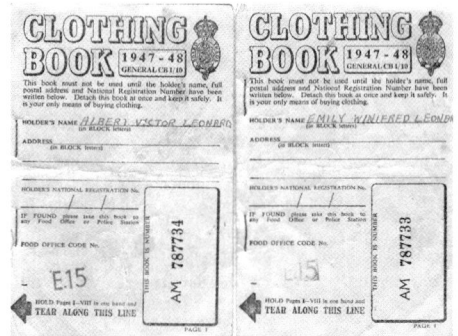

.. You had to bang the hobnails in your boots and things like that because you couldn't get another pair...."
John Dellar *(Oral History Recordings)*

"Clothes were rationed and it was possible to get some on the 'black market', as it was known, without clothing coupons, but how it all happened I have no idea. All I know is being an only child a lot of things were still good and were passed on to my cousins. It was make do and mend as they said and shirt collars were turned round and all sorts of things were made from items no longer used. We had so many clothes coupons allocated and these had to be used carefully."
Marjorie Baker *(Memories of the* War*)*

Women's fashion followed military lines with square shoulders, plain shirts and boxy skirts reflecting their new, more masculine role. It became acceptable for women to wear trousers for all but formal occasions.

The late 1940's style was marked by the return to high fashion and extravagance after the austerity and fabric rationing of the war years. This is best embodied by Christian Dior's 'New Look' silhouette of tailored jacket with nipped in waist and peplum and long, mid-calf length skirt that emphasised the hour-glass silhouette. The new styles required complicated undergarments like garters and girdles to help achieve this look.

Film stars throughout the 1940's had an impact on fashion especially Marlene Dietrich with sexy cocktail dresses and furs, and Katharine Hepburn with her sporty and chic look of high waists and wide-leg trousers. They also influenced the hairstyles of this period.

Soap
All types of soap were rationed. For example in 1945 each person was allocated 4 coupons per month. One coupon would yield 4 oz of hard soap or 6oz of soap powder, for example. Babies and invalids and some workers were allowed more.

Petrol
This was also rationed but in July 1942, the civilian petrol ration was abolished and vehicle fuel was only available for official use, such as buses, farmers, the emergency services, etc. This fuel was dyed for control purposes.

Fuel
Coal was rationed and central heating was banned in the summer months.

Paper
Newsprint was rationed. By 1945, newspapers were limited to 25% of their pre-war consumption. Wrapping paper for most goods was prohibited. Paper shortages meant that schools went short of textbooks.

Shortages

Although not rationed, many items were in short supply, e.g. razor blades, frying pans, baby bottles, alarm clocks etc. etc. Christmas trees were almost impossible to obtain due to timber rationing.

The 'British Restaurant'

Restaurants were not subject to rationing at the start of the war. Well-off people could get round rationing restrictions by eating out frequently.

From May 1942 new restaurant restrictions applied. Meals were restricted to three courses and only one dish could contain fish, game or poultry. No meals could be served between 11.00 p.m. and 5.00 a.m. without a special licence. The maximum price of a meal was set at 5/- (25p). About two thousand *British Restaurants*[2] were run by local authorities in schools and church halls. A simple three course meal cost 9d (about 4p) and no ration coupons were required.

---

[2] *These evolved from the ' Londoners' Meals Service' which was an emergency system for feeding people bombed out of their homes.*

Chapter 11

Wartime Civilian Services and Events

Air Raid Wardens

Back Row (left to right): Francis Webb, Harry Dellar, Bert Worboys.
Front Row: William Alfred Dellar, William George Dellar (Chief Warden), Frank Rayner.

"...... I remember looking at the Doodlebugs going along the back of the church and they used to make a real drumming noise. And then when that stopped you know the bombs was going to be dropped. And one night, I used to get under the table with my teddy bear. Why a teddy bear (laughs)... And Franz Webb, he used to live down by the chapel, he was the Air Raid Warden. And he used to come along ringing his bell, "Raid on! Raid on!", blowing his whistle, and go round. And if there was a crack of light anywhere, bang on your door. He'd say to my mother, "Hilda, you've got a light shining, pull those curtains together." I can hear him saying that now. He was a big old boy wasn't he? Had a cape, and he had a hat, you know... Well it weren't a Trilby, but similar to a Trilby. And he used to come round and of course there was no double glazing and no sound, no lights anywhere. Pitch black, when you went out...... "
Freda Adlington *(Oral History Recordings)*

"..... I can remember the land mine just in front of the 'Green Man' up here, on the hill. I can remember sitting at the top of the hill and seeing a gentleman in army uniform go down into the hole and defuse the bomb (laughs). That wouldn't have been allowed really, but remember father and uncle Bill were wardens so they were there to keep everybody away, and I was allowed to hide in the ditch and watch..... "
John Dellar *- Son of Harry Dellar (Oral History Recordings)*

"......they used to meet in our house. We had a huge table, we had an old fashioned table, and they used to come and sit round, and probably drink tea and stuff. My sister and I had a mattress, one of the old feather mattresses, under the table, and we used to cuddle up under there during the raids, deemed safe, because of the... well, it was quite a sturdy table, which mum had for many years..... "
Muriel Ward *- Daughter of William George Dellar (Oral History Recordings)*

Home Guard

The Home Guard headquarters were in a bungalow in Dubbs Knoll.

Top Row (left to right): *George Cole, Cyril Conder, Tom Harris, Fred Kirbyshire, Jim Woods, Reg Kirbyshire, Bill Webb, Johnny Webb, Dick Covington, Bill Bowden.*
Third Row: *Albert Worboys, George Moule, John Gentle, John Worboys, Jack Matthews, Newton Hunt, Bill Covington, Tom Williams, Tom Leonard, Cyril Izzard, Gordon Gentle.*
Second Row: *Sid Lindsay, Jack Bonnett, Alf Sole, Frank Kirby, Alec Jennings, Eric Anderson, George Reynolds, Bert Thompson, Jim Dellar.*
Front Row: *Sam Stockwell, Cecil Huffer, Fred Law, Tom Watts, Art Law, Fred Bonfield, George Scott.*

In November 1944 the Home Guard organised a very successful Whist Drive, Dance and Dutch Auction to raise money for Christmas presents for fifty five local lads in the Forces. The music for the dance was provided by W. Straten's Band. A grand total of £90 1s 6d was raised.

In July 1945 a Garden Fete was arranged by the Homecoming Fund Committee in the grounds of *'The Cottage'* by kind permission of Major and Mrs Aldridge. Stalls were in the hands of the Home Guard, ARP, NFS, Mother's Union and Red Cross and teas were served by members of the Women's Institute. Children's entertainment was arranged by Mr O Kaye. A Dance was later held in the Village Hall arranged by the ARP. Total proceeds amounted to £102.

".... The Home Guard used to parade in front of the church with broom handles, opposite where the village sign is now. We also used to watch them on manoeuvres jumping in and out of hedges..... "
Peter Wiggett - Evacuee *(Memories of the War)*

Fire Service

The Fire Service was based in a hut in Town Farm. To raise funds for the NFS Benevolent Fund the Fire Service held dances and suppers where the members were often entertained by the Letchworth NFS Band or occasionally by Maurice Rose on the accordion.

Back Row (left to right): *Punch Bonfield, Jack Covington, Lew Hitch, Wally Moss, Bill Darts, Ern Rogers.*
Middle Row: *George Tidy, Jeff Stenton, Sim Starr, Fred Clements, George Merrill.*
Front Row: *Maurice Rose, Billy Conder, Albert Conder, Arthur Dellar, Rupert Dellar, Bill Covington.*
Not Present: *Bill Charter, Billy Miller, Norman Hitch, Will Jarman, Albert Kirbyshire, Pete Thompson, Vic Leonard, Frank Huffer.*

"..... Also we had a fire station in Mr Connor's farmyard where a building was put up for them..... "
Marjorie Baker *(Memories of the War)*

".... My father was a Cambs County Council worker, otherwise known as a Roadman. He travelled miles on his bike keeping ditches and gutters clean. During the war years he was one of the local Fire Brigade whose station was in Connors Yard at the bottom of Church Street, now known as Connors Close. His day job during the war was in an ammunition factory in Baldock which is now Tesco's. Once again he had to cycle there and back each day, then be on call with the Fire Brigade..... "
Barbara Haines *(Memories of the War)*

Red Cross

Guilden Morden Women's Red Cross was part of the Cambridgeshire and Isle of Ely, Arrington II Detachment during the Second World War. The Commandant was Mrs G E Fairchild of the *'Avenels'*. The Assistant was Mrs J Murfitt.

Back Row (left to right): *Kathleen Pratt, Nellie Starr, Doris Starr, Maggie Dellar, Dorothea Price, Elsie Pearce.*
Front Row: *Rose Bonfield, Ivy Dellar, Elizabeth Rayner, Jessie Murfitt, Ida Rule, Marion Lindsay, Marjorie Gentle.*

An ambulance of the type shown here, supplied by the United States, was kept in Harry Dellar's barn. He and Sydney Lindsay were the two designated drivers.

"..... the motorbike and sidecar which was a gift from America and then it turned into the ambulance, which was the big old Dodge ambulance, which we have got a photograph of ... When they did things they had no idea what they were doing. I mean they sent an ambulance to Guilden Morden, well we didn't need an ambulance in the surrounding villages here at all, but they didn't know that. They thought they were doing the right thing, so it came here. But obviously you can't just leave something, so it had to run every fortnight at least, it had to go for a little drive around, so I could go for a ride......"
John Dellar (Oral History Recordings)

In March 1943 the Red Cross organised a special Service in the Parish Church in which the Cambridge Amateur Operatic Society performed. The service was attended by the Home Guard, Fire Service, ARP, British Legion, Guides and

Brownies amongst others, and a guard of honour was formed by the local Red Cross to welcome a large congregation of dignitaries and local people.

BOOK E.

BRITISH RED CROSS SOCIETY.

Founded in 1870.   Incorporated by Royal Charter 1908.

14, Grosvenor Crescent, London, S.W.1.

Register of a*   WOMEN'S   BRITISH RED CROSS DETACHMENT.
(*State here whether Men's, Women's or Mixed)

Name of County Branch *Cambs · Isle of Ely*.   Registered No. of Detachment /118 ·

Division of County Organizing Detachment *Arrington II*

Name of Commandant *Mrs Fairchild*

Full Address   "*Avenels*"

                              Guilden Morden.

Telephone No. *Steeple Morden* 262 .

INSTRUCTIONS FOR KEEPING BOOK E

1. It is the duty of the Commandant to see that the records of all personnel are entered in this book, and that the records are up to date and accurate. This book is a permanent record, and must be handed on to succeeding Commandants. In no circumstances should any of the records of present or past members ever be destroyed.
2. When a member is transferred Record Sheet A should accompany the transfer form.
3. When a member is discharged his/her Record Sheet A should be forwarded to the County Office with the Discharge Form E 7 and Form D(8).
4. At the end of the detachment year (31st October) two copies of Form E(4) should be filled in and forwarded with this Book to the County Director by registered post. The County Director will sign and return this book to the Commandant when the records have been checked.
5. The Record Sheets A should be kept in alphabetical order, working from the front of the book.
   The Record Sheets B should be kept in yearly order, working from the back of the book.
6. (a) Section 1 of Record Sheet A, columns K, N, Q, T, should be used for any of the remaining Society's examinations, keeping the same subject under one column.
   (b) Section 1 of Record Sheet A, columns headed Proficiency Badge, Bars or Failures, should be entered: P—Prof. Badge; B—Bars; F—Failures. P and B should only be entered when the badge or bar is obtained from Headquarters.
   (c) Section 2 of Record Sheet A: Special qualifications held by members with details of certificates or diplomas should be entered here.

Royal British Legion

There was an ex-servicemen's club in existence in Guilden Morden which joined the newly formed British Legion in 1921 and maintained a membership of around forty five. The Branch was responsible for sending members to convalescent homes, providing coal for elderly and widowed people and taking care of the War Memorial. They were also prominent in raising funds for the new Village Hall built in 1927.

At the end of the Second World War the Branch organised a sale of poppies to celebrate Armistice Day which raised over £20, a fair sum in those days, which was forwarded to Earl Haig's Fund. In the evening a gathering was held in the Village Hall with returned POW Private Cecil Sole as guest of honour, the refreshments being provided by Don Beale of the Bull Hotel, Royston. Toasts were given in the famous Sandeman Port, a gift of the patron of the Branch, Major Pat Sandeman of Morden House.

The following day a United Service was held in the Parish Church when the names of the fallen were read out by the Branch Secretary Mr W J Gentle. This is an event which is continued to this day alternating between Guilden Morden and Steeple Morden churches.

The Guilden Morden and Steeple Morden Branches are currently merged to form the Mordens Branch. They are backed up by a very active Women's Section.

Chapter 12

Evacuees

Many evacuees came to Guilden Morden during the war years. Some came individually, usually because of some previous connection with the village. Others were 'official' evacuees, who came as part of the government's initiative to relocate children away from the large towns. The main group in this category was the children from the Hungerford Road School, Islington who came with some of their teachers. Another group were the elderly ladies who were residents in a Nursing Home that was relocated from London to Morden House.

The following are the written and recorded recollections of some of our evacuees.

Peter Wiggett

"My memories of the war years at Guilden Morden from age 3 to 9 (1939-1945)"

"I came home from school one day and Mrs Gordon, my guardian, said she had a knock on the door and it was an Italian prisoner of war. He asked if he could borrow a bicycle (she had a big sit-up-and-beg type of bike). The reason being he had slashed his arm with a sickle and wanted to go to Ashwell for treatment. She said yes and it was returned in due course. The Italian prisoners had been trimming mangels just up the road. On the odd occasion Mrs Gordon would take me by bus to Royston on Saturdays. She would always buy fishcakes on the market before a visit to the Priory Cinema. One film I recall was 'Anchors Aweigh' and of course the Pathe News. The bus would travel through Litlington US airbase which was on both sides of the road. On one of the trips the bus was stopped and a very big US MP came on the bus, a woman's voice rang out 'we are all English here', and the MP saluted and said 'carry on mam'. As a little lad of five or six he scared me with his guns and truncheon and big white helmet (they called the MPs 'snowdrops').The bus was usually full of women and a few children. Many times we would see the US Flying Fortresses overhead going out, and later we would see them return with props missing or not working and bits shot off the wings etc. We also watched hundreds of planes towing gliders, the gliders always seemed to be at an angle behind the towing plane, this must have been the Arnhem attack.

Guilden Morden was always very quiet most of the time, so at any unusual noise I would rush out to see what it was. I heard this noise coming from the direction of Ashwell, so I went out to look and could not believe my eyes. It was a tank and other vehicles. I went and called Mrs Gordon, then ran out into the road as they had stopped outside our house. I went and had a good look and was most disappointed as it was a Jeep covered in cardboard or similar material, all painted up to look like a tank. This must have been just before the invasion of France.

A friend called to tell me there was a gun just up the road, so up the road we went to see this anti-aircraft gun. There were two soldiers with it and they let us sit on it and turn the handle to move it up and down. We got into trouble with the soldiers because we had muddy boots on and had to get off in a hurry. They then took us into a big barn nearby with other soldiers. They were brewing up with a fire in the middle of the floor. The soldier sitting next to me gave me a piece of chocolate, it was the first piece I can remember eating. I went home and Mrs Gordon scolded me for eating a soldier's rations."

Evacuees in 1944
Back Row (left to right): Lily Treen (nee (Wiggett and her baby), Esther Gordon (who took in Peter and Douglas Wiggett), Douglas Wiggett, Connie Wiggett and her baby. **Middle Row:** Dorothy Mence. **Front Row:** Jean Mence, Milly Bullock, Peter Wiggett (on his 8th birthday), Teddy Bullock.

Sheila Woodbridge (nee Cross) from Thornley, Western Australia

"I was almost ten years old at the start of WW2. I distinctly remember gathering at the school playground at Hungerford Road School in Islington, London. I wondered why parents and children were crying, all had been explained to me by my foster parents, and I felt that this was my great adventure! After a long train and bus ride, I arrived at Guilden Morden, coming to rest in the village school, where we were taken one by one to the good folk of the village, to be billeted. I was given a home by May and Bert Seymour and their small son Kenneth at 1 Avenel Terrace, this turned out to be one of the best times of my life, Mrs Seymour made me so welcome in her two up - two down cottage. In spite of no running water, no electricity, the kitchen range for cooking, candles and oil lamps for lighting, (a plain one for the kitchen, and prettier one for the tiny front room), I was extremely happy. Kenneth had moved into his parents' bedroom so I could enjoy the other room. I was intrigued to find the stairs behind what appeared to be a cupboard door.

Mrs Seymour was a good cook, my first meal was lamb chops with new potatoes and fresh peas, delicious! I remember her putting eggs in water glass in a bucket for cake cooking etc., the postman used to sometimes bring Kenny and me nice brown new laid eggs, which we often found on the doorstep! There was apple or plum pie on Sunday usually fruit that had fallen off the farmers' trees. Water was dragged in buckets from the end of ten cottages. You needed arms like a navvy to use the pump! The pump used to get frozen in the winter, so water had to be collected before nightfall, some left on the kitchen range all night, so the pump could be defrosted with hot water the next day.

The toilet was a rather primitive chemical affair, in the barn at the end of the yard. After I had lived there for a while, two taps were installed to be shared by ten cottages! Also electricity was laid on and there was a great deal of complaint about the rents going up from 5 shillings (25p) to 7/6d (37.5p) per week to cover the cost!

Bert Seymour had an allotment and one of my joys was to help him dig and cut vegetables and bring them home. We also kept rabbits and we would go round the hedgerows collecting rabbit food after school. School was held in the village hall. Next to the school was 'the rec.' including cricket pitch, where I spent many happy hours after school with lemonade and sandwiches supplied by May. We used to play on a rusty old roller which had shafts for a horse. Bath nights would seem incredible in today's world. Friday night the zinc bath was hauled up from the barn, set in front of the fire with a blanket draped over the clotheshorse to keep out the draughts! The water had been heating up on the range all day, first in, Kenneth, then me, followed by May, and Bert last! May Seymour found my clothes inadequate, so she cleverly cut down clothing and made me a hat, coat and dress for Sunday church, riches indeed! Kenneth was a lovely little boy with a mop of auburn curls. I also recall her hemming nappies for Mrs Izzard.

May was active in cleaning and polishing in the village church. I joined the choir and the Brownies supervised by Miss Price, the Vicar's unmarried daughter. I recall she played the church organ and one piece of music I remember very clearly. When I hummed it to my husband, he said it is a piece by Bach, 'Sleepers Awake'. I suppose it was appropriate for Rev. Price's sermons! I took the Rev. Price to task for calling my friend U-nice-ee, (Eunice). He said "that is how it is said in the Bible", and I cheekily asked how he knew! Mrs Seymour taught me to embroider simple stitches in coloured cottons. This has been a life-long love and I have been teaching embroidery for some years now. One of my jobs was to take the accumulator (which ran the radio) to Steeple Morden for filling and re-charging, with strict instructions not to swing it around because it contained acid. It was quite a long walk. I recall seeing the Italian POW's working in the fields on the way. The Seymour's had friends in Steeple Morden (I think at the pub), the daughters name was Avis.

Life in an English country village was a revelation to me after the grime and hectic life of London, I embraced everything about country living and found it very much to my liking.

Pea-picking - what memories that evokes! All the pickers in a long line stretched right across the field of peas, we all took a low stool to sit on, plus a bucket with lemonade and something to eat, we would work our way through the field grabbing and uprooting a bunch of peas - pulling off the fat peas only, we had to fill four large buckets to fill a sack, which was weighed to make sure it was full, for that we got the princely sum of one shilling (5p) per sack! One day we came across a field full of peas and thistles, we all went on strike for more pay, our hands likely to be very sore and even bleeding, our wages got doubled to two shillings per sack! I earned 21 shillings for my efforts over a school holiday. This enabled me to buy Christmas presents for my Mum and other relatives living in or near London. I remember May picking cowslips or 'Peggles' as the locals called them, wrapping them in a damp cloth and posting them off to my aunt in London to give her a taste of Spring from the country. When the land mine fell at the end of the village, many children rushed there to pick up the largest piece of shrapnel they could find. The war brought gas mask drill, maps in school classrooms with rows of swastikas and union jacks showing the position of the troops. We also spent time in our teacher's garden 'digging for victory' planting vegetables and soft fruits. In school we painstakingly knitted scarves and socks for the troops and sent them away with little love notes in the toe of the socks.

I loved the smells in the village shop, of candles and lamp oil among spices etc. I believe the shop was near the blacksmiths forge, where we used to pump the bellows for him and watch the horseshoes being made and fitted, and sometimes new rims on cartwheels.

In the winter months ponds got frozen over and the village children skated on skilfully made wooden blades attached to their boots. The summer seemed endless, with wild flowers in abundance, the smell of new mown hay and ripening fruit on the trees. 'Conkers' was a favourite game from the lovely old chestnut trees in the village.

I was successful in the 11-plus exam, and had to move on to Grammar School and a different environment in St Albans. I have never forgotten my life in Guilden Morden, although it was short-lived. It was definitely the best time I had as an evacuee.

Frederick Saker – 'An Evacuee's Tale'

"The United Kingdom declared war on Germany on September 1st 1939, but the government decided that the evacuation of children, from the major towns at risk of being bombed should begin on September 1st. Thus it was that early on that morning I found myself among several hundred other youngsters (I was three months away from my 8th birthday), assembled at a North London tube station, to be taken to Kings Cross and from thence to an 'unknown destination.' Neither the tearful parents, nor the team of 'dispatchers' knew where we would end up by the end of that day. Each child was required to wear a brown-paper label, strung around the neck, showing their name and, in my case, the word 'solo', as I was not accompanied by siblings. There were two other adornments: a brown cardboard box, also on a string, containing a gas-mask - a nasty, stifling contraption smelling of cheap rubber - and a paper bag (plastic ones did not exist then) containing an orange, a bar of chocolate and a comic. The steam train - exciting for us all - eventually deposited about 50 of us at Royston, from where about 12 of us were transported by coach - in those days known as 'charabancs' - to Manor Farm in Shingay where, having been given a welcome glass of fizz, we were told to line up under a huge old tree to await the arrival of the local kind people who had elected to take an evacuee. And so they arrived and, moving along the line, selected a boy or girl to take home.

To my great dismay, and on the verge of tears, I was the last to be picked, but how lucky I was that a lovely lady, Mrs Beatrice Mynott, took the risk of 'adopting' this little London rascal who, even in that moment, had hopes of catching his first rabbit. About 9 months later, after the period of what was called the 'phoney war' there had been no significant bombing of London and so the majority of the evacuees had returned home to their parents. In my case, having taken to country life like a duck to water, I remained happily in Shingay for nearly four years before, following a form of 11-plus exam, I was sent to further my education in Bury St. Edmunds in Suffolk.

On September 1st 1939 in a period of about 4 hours, I went from a world of central-heating, water from the tap, electric light at the flick of a switch, and a lavatory which flushed at the pull of a chain, to a humble farm-worker's cottage which possessed none of those comforts. In fact, one of my morning tasks before beginning the walk to school in

Guilden Morden, was to don a small wooden yoke and fetch two heavy buckets of water from the age-old spring, which then existed in Shingay. Another of my domestic duties was to regularly dig a hole in the Mynott's garden, and empty the bucket from the ivy-covered outhouse at the end of the garden path. Thus I learned that tomato seeds pass through the human body, and develop hardy plants with an excellent yield of fruit...

School in Guilden Morden was good fun - in spite of the long walk there and back which in winter winds was, for a young kid in short trousers, a character forming experience. I made good friends there and I still remember some of their names, especially a pretty girl called Betty Tidy. The headmistress was Miss Still and I still possess a book prize she awarded to me 'for a very good diary while evacuated to Guilden Morden'. She lived in a bungalow with the name of Windy Ridge, I seem to recall.

Such strong memories, which will never leave me, of leading a horse at harvest time.....pea-picking, potato-lifting.....going out with the grown-ups on shoots on frosty mornings, acting as gun-dog to retrieve, and humanely despatch, wounded birds, rabbits and hares. Hanging around the 'drum' at threshing time, trying to kill the mice fleeing the sheaves, so that the numerous local cats would be well-nourished. The deceased, bleeding, creatures would be stored in my jacket pocket which would consequently acquire a most pungent smell. Next morning the residual odour would be remarked on by the teachers, and I was made to hand (over) the offending garment in an outhouse.

At Manor Farm - one of four owned by the Bath family - I earned a few pennies on summer evenings by weeding the garden. This employment came to an end after it was discovered that I frequently made my way into the cattle-sheds in order to scoop up with my hands the thick black treacle kept in open barrels there, which formed part of the animals' diet. Forbidden fruit but delicious! At South Farm, in a barn which still exists today, there lived four German prisoners of war. They were 'trusties' from the POW camp at Royston, who were allowed to live-out, and were employed on the local farms. On many evenings I would walk to their barn, share with them their potato-soup and thus learned my first words in their language. I still have the notes which they made for me at the time and, much later in life, acquired a very good grasp of German which greatly helped me when I launched myself on the world as an export consultant.

How much I could add to the foregoing.......how long I could hope to hold the attention of anyone willing to listen!"

Don Mackarsie – 'Working on a small farm in the 1940's'

Don Mackarsie (b.28.4.30) arrived in Guilden Morden from his home in London in September 1940 as an evacuee. He came with his mother who was able to work in a nursing home which had relocated to Morden House in Guilden Morden. Don's father remained in London working as an ARP Warden before joining his family when the war ended. Initially accommodation for Don and his mother was provided at the nursing home but she left after nine months on account of the poor management and running of the nursing home. So they moved to a council property before living in Somborne Cottage in Church Street. The land surrounding Morden House had been purchased by Mr D J Thompson in 1941 but he lived outside the village at Redhill, near Buntingford, some 7 miles away. His holding in 1941 was 34 acres with 13 cows and calves and one horse. Don recalls as a lad of 11 watching hay-making and wanting to 'have a go' which led to a weekend job until he left school. This was the start of his career in farming and henceforth Don was always known as 'Bert' by Mr Thompson! After he left school aged 15 he was unable to pursue his wish to study engineering in a technical college in Cambridge as places were all filled, so he applied for work with Mr Thompson.

By this time Mr Thompson had 12-15 milking cows with "followers" (calves), and it was Don's job at the age of 16 yrs to look after the animals in every respect, including the milking. Mr Thompson was interested in modern techniques and had built a modern milking shed with electricity and milking machines. He had built up his pedigree herd of Friesians (the Morden Herd) using good bulls. At the time he was 'one of the leading lights' for artificial insemination in the country.

Although milking machines were used in the dairy, for a time the cows were milked by hand as this technique was considered to be best for the animals, but it was hard work and a much slower task, so milking by machine was resumed. All the milk was sold in bulk to Saggers Dairy in Bassingbourn The other dairy in Guilden Morden was at Murfitt's Farm. They had a large dairy herd and delivered bottled milk in the village, including to the village school and shops, but when another company (name not known) ceased milk deliveries in the village, Thompson's took over their round with Don using a 3-wheeled bicycle for the job. All the milk then was bottled on the farm and was stored in a tank prior to being transferred to a cooling tank (by cold flowing water). The milk from there then went to another tank from which the milk was piped into four bottles, two at a time. 50 – 60 gallons of milk were produced a day. Sterilization of bottles and equipment took place using chemicals. During the war land girls ran the bottling plant and after the war local people were employed until 1957 when milk production reverted to bulk sale and the round was sold to the Co-op. Pig production with 200 animals was also part of Mr Thompson's farm. They were sold at the weekly Monday market in Cambridge and also to Playles of Litlington. Animals were transported by Mr Savage of Steeple Morden in his cattle lorry (there were two brothers: one ran the garage and taxi business; the other, animal transportation).

As with other farms during the war Thompson's farm employed two land girls, Isobel Dobson came from Newcastle and lived in a hostel for land girls at Glebe House in Wendy (Don found her Geordie accent almost impossible to understand!) and the other, Vera Furley, was working in Cornwall but her mother who lived in Guilden Morden asked if she could be employed locally. A German Prisoner of War, Gunther also worked on the farm. He was brought in by lorry from his camp on Royston Heath. There were 200-300 POWs in the camp at this time.

In the notoriously bad winter of 1947 Mr Thompson was unable to reach his farm from his home for nearly a week as snow drifts were 11ft deep at Ashwell Station where Mr Thompson would have needed to cross the road leading to Guilden Morden, so the farm work was undertaken by Don, Peter Elborough (a maths teacher between jobs) working for 3 months on the milk round and Isobel and Vera. Don recalls that due to the cold it took longer to open the milking house than to milk the cows - they were all right as they were in a covered yard. Mr Thompson eventually purchased Morden House and Morden House Farm in its entirety in 1947. As well as a dairy herd and pig production, cereal crops were *grown. The first combine harvester in the area after the war was bought by Mr Pepper (later Clayton farms) but the smallholders and small farms in the area would use 'threshing tackle' (a variety of machines) provided by Mr Newton Hunt, the farmer at North Brook End, to gather in their harvest. Don describes his relationship with Mr Thompson as a very good one – he had been given responsibility at an early age and been entrusted to take on all tasks required on a small farm at this time giving him all-round experience for general farming. He eventually had his own farm in Guilden Morden."*

Source: From an interview by the Guilden Morden Local History Group

Margaret Stevens (nee Mclean)

Two million children left the towns and cities as evacuees on September 1st 1939. They did not know where they were going, but were put on trains and were told they would have new homes in the safety of the countryside. Among them was Margaret Stevens, who returned to Guilden Morden on the sixtieth anniversary of her evacuation after travelling the world and said: *"I still like this place the best."* Margaret was only eight when she was put on the train from London to Cambridge on September 1st 1939. The children were given a brown paper bag containing chocolate, biscuits, a tin of corned beef and a couple of rolls, and taken in a convoy of double-decker buses to be dropped off across the country. She was set down with her suitcase, gas mask and luggage label pinned to her coat with thirty other children at almost the last stop, Guilden Morden, and taken in by bakers Sid and Marion Lindsay.

Her first impression was favourable. On the back seat of the car was a large tray of cakes and she was told to help herself. From then on she called the Lindsays, Uncle Sid and Auntie Marion and spent three happy years in the village. *"I loved it and was very happy. I had lots of fun in the bake house and I didn't want to go back to London."* she said. *"The freedom here was unbelievable."*

But when Margaret was eleven she was told she had to go back to grammar school in Islington as Cambridgeshire schools would not take evacuees. But she hated London and the bombing and in 1944 ran back to Guilden Morden and stayed all summer. She said *"Ever since, I have taken every opportunity to come back. I wish I had come back straight after the war."*

Her first husband was a merchant seaman so she lived around the world, Ghana, previously called the Gold Coast, Nigeria and Libya. She now lives with husband Ian in Suffolk and says she is too settled to move to Guilden Morden.

Sid Lindsay died in 1972 after a road accident, and Auntie Marion passed away in 1991, but Margaret still keeps in touch with her then best friends Muriel Dellar and Lindsay Lindsay, daughter of Sid and Marion.

Source: The Royston Crow. The photo of Margaret with Lindsay is by Neville Chuck.

Morden House

During January 1940 some thirty female residents of an old people's home in London were evacuated to Guilden Morden and were accommodated in Morden House together with their Matron, Miss Doris Wilcock. The Rector used to visit them and hold services for them.

" ...we were with the vicar and we used to sing....give them a little sing-song and a Service, they used to look forward to that..."
Freda Adlington (Oral History Recordings)

Unfortunately, between March 1940 and January 1945 at least fifteen of these ladies passed away and were buried in the village cemetery. There were complaints at a Parish Council meeting that these burials of people from outside the parish were taking up too much space in the village cemetery!

In 1941, the Matron was charged with four offences of obtaining money by false pretences. She appeared before magistrates at Arrington Police Court and evidence was brought concerning the drawing of pensions of residents who had previously died and of claiming a billeting allowance for a resident who had left the home. The defendant was found guilty on all four counts and was fined a total of £20

Apparently the Matron also hired out rooms to some other visitors. No doubt this was a lucrative sideline!

" ... she also looked after the young ladies that used to come over for the Americans... She used to put them up, because the Americans had got money and they paid for them...But she put them (i.e. the elderly residents)... all together (in one room) in the wartime, so she could make room for these young ladies that used to come over..."
Freda Adlington (Oral History Recordings)

Chapter 13

Those Who Served

Those who did not survive

Albert Percy Worboys - Private in the Suffolk Regiment. Died 31st May 1940 in Belgium aged 21. He is buried in De Panne Communal Cemetery, Belgium. Albert was the son of William Percy and Hannah Worboys of Guilden Morden.

Geoffrey Edward Rayner - Died 15th April 1942 aged 19. Geoffrey was the son of Frank and Elizabeth Rayner of Guilden Morden. He had been a draughtsman at Kryn and Lahy, Letchworth, had received lower grades for the army than he had expected and while the balance of his mind was disturbed, took his own life.

Douglas Waldock - Trooper in the Queens Own Royal West Kent Regiment, Reconnaissance Corps. Died 29th April 1943 in Tunisia aged 26. Douglas was born 1916 in Ashwell, the son of Owen George and Flora Waldock. He married Ethel Kirbyshire in 1936 in Guilden Morden and they had two children. He is buried in Enfidaville War Cemetery, Sousse, Tunisia.

Frederick George Dowdy - Private in the Queens Royal Regiment (West Surrey). Died 29th October 1943 in Italy aged 29. Frederick was the son of Thomas and Annie Dowdy of Guilden Morden. He is buried in Minturno War Cemetery, Italy.

Sidney Turnell - Private in the Royal Army Medical Corps. Died 10th January 1944 in Italy aged 35. Sidney was the son of Ernest and Jessica Turnell and the husband of Mabel Fanny. He is buried in Bari War Cemetery, Italy

Leonard Francis Webb - Flight Sergeant, Navigator, Wireless Operator and Air Gunner in the Royal Air Force Voluntary Reserve. Lost 28th April 1944 over France aged 21. Leonard was the son of Albert and Jessie Webb of Guilden Morden. His Halifax was lost with all crew whilst carrying out a raid on a marshalling yard and is buried in Maubeuge-Centre Cemetery, France.

Richard Strickland Westrope - Sergeant, Flight Engineer in the Royal Air Force Voluntary Reserve. Died 29th July 1944 in Germany aged 21. Richard was the son of Herbert John Wright and Agnes Lilian Westrope of Husborne Crawley, Bedfordshire and is buried in Kiel War Cemetery, Germany.

Bernard Frank Bonfield - Signalman in the Royal Corps of Signals. Died 25th June 1945 in Germany aged 24. 'Bernie' as he was known was the son of Frank and Kate Bonfield of the *'Black Horse'* Public House. He died in Germany as the result of accidental gunshot wounds and is buried in Hamburg Cemetery.

John Edward Davis - Gunner in the Royal Artillery 135 (The Hertfordshire Yeomanry) Field Regiment. Died 19th August 1945 in Thailand aged 29. John died after an attack of dysentery and malaria whilst a Japanese prisoner of war and is buried in Kanchanaburi War Cemetery, Thailand. He had lived with his sister Mrs Steel in Guilden Morden after the death of his mother in 1935.

Sylvia Joan Leete - Private in the Auxiliary Territorial Service. Died 1945 of TB at the age of 25. She was the daughter of Cecil Wynn and Emily Jeanette Leete. They are all buried in Guilden Morden Cemetery. It is said that she came home on leave where she fell ill. Her father refused to let her return to her base, but the Military Police came and fetched her. She was admitted to hospital (in Colchester?) suffering from TB. She died at Chalkdell Hospital in Baldock. She is listed on the Guilden Morden and the Baldock War Memorials, but as of June 2013 is not accepted for commemoration as war dead.

Those who survived

Tony Christy - Pilot in the Royal Air Force. Tony lived in Ashwell before settling in Guilden Morden.

Elsie Colley (nee Worboys) - Private in the Auxiliary Territorial Service. Elsie was the daughter of Alfred John and Elizabeth Worboys. She joined the ATS in 1940 having previously worked for Messrs Falk at the Embroidery Works in Letchworth.

Francis Edward Colley - Frank joined the army in 1941 as a Gunner. He came from Stoke-on-Trent where he worked for the LMS Railway. He married Elsie Worboys (above) in 1941.

Cecil Jack Dellar - Jack served in a Royal Air Force Operational Training Group in the Bahamas. He was the son of William Alfred and Florence Dellar. He married three times after the war and had two sons. He died in 1986 in Stevenage.

Maurice Fred Dennis - Private in the Beds and Herts Regiment. Maurice was born in Potton, the son of Mrs and Mrs F Dennis, later of Valley Farm. He married Phyllis Huffer whilst on leave in 1943. He died in 1986.

Ernest Henry Dore - Private in the Beds and Herts Regiment. Ernie was born in London. He married Elizabeth Merrill in 1942 and played football for Guilden Morden. He died in 1989.

Sidney John Gentle - Flight Lieutenant in the Royal Air Force.

Neville John Godman - Private in the Army. Neville was the son of John and Winifred Godman. He married Brenda Darby in 1943 in Guilden Morden.

Jack Harrington - Staff Sergeant in the Army. Jack originated from Ireland. He married Lilian Sole in 1940.

Debbie Hawkins - Private in the Auxiliary Territorial Service. Debbie was a convoy driver during the war.

Albert Kirbyshire - Driver in the Royal Army Service Corps. Alf, as he was best known, was the son of Arthur and Martha Kirbyshire. He married Evelyn Sadler in 1947 in Norfolk. He died in 2000 and his cremated remains are in Guilden Morden Cemetery.

Charles William Lilley - Driver in the Royal Army Service Corps. Charley was the son of John William and Naomi Lilley. He married Audrey Thompson in 1948 in Cambridge and they had three children. He died in 1998 in Lister Hospital, Stevenage and is buried in Guilden Morden Cemetery.

Elsie Manning - Women's Auxiliary Air Force. Elsie was the daughter of Mr and Mrs Joseph Manning of High Street, Guilden Morden. She served at an aerodrome in the Home Counties.

Alfred William Mynott - Royal Air Force. Alf, son of Henry and Beatrice Mynott of Shingay, married Phyllis Peckett in 1940 and had one son. He died in 2001.

Arthur Claude Pearce - Company Sergeant Major in the Royal Army Service Corps. Claude married Kathleen Millns in 1941. He became landlord of the *'Three Tuns'* Public House in 1950.

Cecil Watts - Private in the Suffolk Regiment. Cecil was the eldest son of Fred and Lizzie Watts. He died in 1990 in Addenbrookes Hospital and is buried in Guilden Morden Cemetery.

Stanley Watts - The Devonshire Regiment. Stanley was the youngest son of Fred and Lizzie Watts. He married Irene Harding in 1948. He died in Guilden Morden in 1994 and is buried in the Cemetery.

Maurice Worboys - The Northamptonshire Regiment. 'Mig', as he was known, was the son of Charles and Harriet Worboys of Abington Pigotts. He married Cynthia Peckett in 1959. He died in a road accident in 1987 and is buried in Guilden Morden Cemetery.

Stanley Worboys - Gunner. Stan was the son of Fanny Worboys. He married Edna Watts in 1942.

Japanese Prisoners of War who survived

Leslie Charles Worboys

Private in the Cambridgeshire Regiment. Les was the son of William Percy and Hannah Worboys. News of Private Worboys was reported in the Royston Crow on 14th July 1944. Les died in 2000 at the White House, Steeple Morden and was cremated at Cambridge Crematorium.

'Mr and Mrs P Worboys received news on Saturday last of their youngest son, twenty-four-year-old Pte L C Worboys who is a prisoner of war in Japanese hands. Pte Worboys was reported missing at the fall of Singapore, two and a half years ago, and this is the first news his parents have received from him.' (Royston Crow)

Cecil Charles Edward Sole

Private in the Cambridgeshire Regiment. Cecil was the son of Alfred and Maud Sole. News of his capture was reported in the Royston Crow on 14th January 1944. Cecil had joined the RAF VR in January having previously been employed by the Royston and District Laundry Co. Ltd as a van driver. He married Betty Cosford, a nurse at Morden House, in 1946. At the Armistice Celebrations in Guilden Morden in November 1945 Cecil was the guest of honour. He died in 1958 aged 37 in Huntingdon County Hospital after a road accident.

'Mr and Mrs Sole, 8 Council Houses, Guilden Morden, have received news of their son, Pte C Sole, 1st Cambs Regiment, the first news since the fall of Singapore. Pte Sole stated in the card that he is interred in No.1 P.O.W. Camp, Thailand and is in excellent health, and working for pay.' (Royston Crow)

Chapter 14

Steeple Morden and Bassingbourn Airfields

During the war years the people of Guilden Morden were greatly affected by the presence of the two local airfields at Steeple Morden and Bassingbourn. The sight and sound of aircraft in the skies over the village left an indelible memory on those who were there. It had the effect of bringing the war closer to home.

"I remember my parents and the neighbours would stand and count the planes leaving Bassingbourn Camp and then count them home in the morning to see how many made it home and what parts were missing from the planes."
Barbara Haines (*Written Memories*)

There were also many flying accidents that occurred in the area, some of which are detailed below. Local people often observed these dramatic events and the resulting wreckage.

" that (a cartridge) was from a Mustang that crashed at the back of Bury Home Farm. And well I actually saw that come down. We were on our bikes, and down there to the site, and we was there before the Americans got there from Litlington ....and warned off out .... and told to get out of the way, because of ammunition exploding ..."
Don Mackarsie (*Oral History Recordings*)

There was also the presence and contact with the military personnel from the airfields. At the peak there were two thousand airmen and support staff at Steeple Morden and over four thousand at Bassingbourn. Some of the Americans may have seemed a little larger than life.

"There was a Sergeant Johnson, who was (stationed at) Towlers Corner[1] at Litlington, when the Americans were here. He used to come over and ... my father was a teetotaller right ...but Sergeant Johnson used to get drunk every time he came over, but he would give my father the keys to his jeep, because he was Military Police and he would give the keys and the rotary arm, which he would take out of his jeep to my father, by the end of the evening he would be fast asleep in the corner of the village hall. My father would help him out and get him in the car, and get him home. He would sleep on the settee, or if you like the chaise longue in the sitting room, and about three or four o'clock in the morning he would wake up, and he would take his keys and his rotary arm back to the village hall, and get his jeep and go back home, back to Towlers Corner. And he got so friendly, and he did it so many times, of course he... he turned up in the day time sometimes and he would bring cans of ice cream, and cans of peaches and things like that..."
John Dellar (*Oral History Recordings*):

---

[1] Many American servicemen were housed in accommodation at Towlers Corner, Litlington.

Steeple Morden Airfield
Construction
The airfield, initially a satellite of RAF Bassingbourn, was built by John Laing & Son on land owned by George Jarman, George Smyth and Bert Parrish.

An Early Event
In 1939 a Hurricane pilot dazzled by the searchlight near the farm shop at Beverley Farm bailed out and his plane crashed near the Steeple Morden church.

RAF
In May 1940, 11 OTU (Operational Training Unit) was formed and was to operate from Bassingbourn and Steeple Morden. They flew Wellingtons (pictured) and Ansons – one hundred aircraft in total. RAF personnel were billeted in Steeple Morden and Litlington.

Some of the incidents that occured at the airfield from 1940 to 1942
A Wellington hit a steamroller being used for construction of one of the runways.

Another on take-off hit a parked Wellington and burst into flames, with loss of life.

A new Wellington, donated by the people of Birmingham, overshot a shortened runway under construction and was a total loss after flying for only five hours.

A German intruder shot down a Wellington on the crew's first night flight. The plane came down on the airfield but the pilots were unhurt.

Two pupil pilots on a night solo flight were shot down on their approach to land. The aircraft was on fire but landed in a nearby field with the crew unhurt.

A Wellington, practicing how to get out of a stall, plummeted to earth, with the loss of everyone on board.

On the night of 14/15 November 1940 three bombs were dropped on the airfield. There was no damage or injury.

On 16 February 1941 a German Ju88 landed at Steeple Morden after being damaged while on a bombing raid on Liverpool. The crew were captured and the plane was taken to Farnborough for investigation.

On the night of 26 February 1941 Steeple Morden airfield was attacked and ten bombs were dropped and the airfield machine gunned. Two Wellingtons were slightly damaged. One of the ground gunners received two bullets through his helmet knocking him out but he was unhurt.

On the night of 10 April 1941 ten high explosive bombs were dropped on the airfield. Only one exploded, injuring an airman. A further eight bombs and incendiaries were dropped later that night.

On 10 April 1941 a Wellington was shot down by an unidentified enemy aircraft. It crashed and burnt out near Ashwell Station, pilot and pupil escaping injury.

Eight days later a Wellington crashed at Abington Pigotts, killing both crew members.

On 29 April 1941 a lone bomber dropped a 50kg bomb on the airfield and thirteen days later the airfield was again attacked and twelve high explosive bombs were dropped.

On 7 May 1941 a Wellington made a forced landing at Wendy after being attacked by a Ju88.

On 5 June 1941 bombs cratered No.2 runway.

On 9 June 1941 a Wellington that took off from Steeple Morden was lost over the North Sea with the loss of the crew of seven.

On 8 July 1941 a Wellington crashed at Litlington, killing the crew of three.

On 18 July 1941 a Wellington attempting to land was machine gunned by a Ju88.

On 22 July 1941 a Wellington with eight crew collided with a Ju88 with three crew over Ashwell Church. The aircraft exploded in a ball of flame, with wreckage falling at the edge of Ashwell and the tail of the Ju88 in Ashwell High Street. All eleven airmen lost their lives.

On August Bank Holiday 1941 a string of incendiary bombs fell on Rectory Farm, Guilden Morden, causing considerable damage. Alec Jennings was the farmer at the time and saved two bombs that failed to ignite and made them safe.

On 4 September 1941 the airfield was bombed by a British Blenheim bomber dropping two bombs (rumoured to be a plane captured by the Germans).

In February 1942 two Wellingtons were lost on training exercises with the loss of twelve air crew.

'1,000 Bomber Raids' – May/June 1942

For this, the first of the '1,000 bomber raids', it was necessary to bring together aircraft from all sources including the Operational Training Units. '11 OTU' were to contribute twenty five Wellingtons (twelve from Bassingbourn and thirteen from Steeple Morden).

On 31 May 1942 one thousand and forty six aircraft took off for Cologne. From the OTUs it was mainly instructors who piloted the aircraft with trainees making up the rest of the crew. The raid was a success. One of the Wellingtons from Steeple Morden was lost. The next night on 1 June, a raid on Essen took place. This raid was not successful and one of eleven aircraft from Steeple Morden did not return.

On 25 June there was another raid, this time on Bremen. Although the target was covered in cloud, it was considered a success. However, of thirteen aircraft from Steeple Morden, three were lost.

Other wartime details

The land mine that landed in the field next to Trap Road, Guilden Morden produced a crater the size of a house. Also incendiary bombs dropped close to Cheney Water Farm started numerous fires but little damage was done.

Morden House was earmarked for an emergency mortuary for surrounding villages but it was never needed.

USAAF

The 355th Fighter Group were formed in November 1942 in Orlando, Florida. After training, the airmen were shipped across the Atlantic and arrived in Steeple Morden in early July 1943. They were followed by the first aircraft to arrive, P-47 Thunderbolts (pictured right).

On 6 September 1943 RAF Steeple Morden was handed over formally to the USAAF. The 355th flew combat missions virtually daily from September 1943 to April 1945. Their role was to escort bombers on raids on enemy targets, but the range of the Thunderbolts was not sufficient for the longer trips and losses were too heavy when the bombers were beyond fighter escort. A new long range fighter was required.

In the Spring of 1944 the first P-51B Mustangs fitted with Rolls Royce engines arrived. These had a range of 750 miles when fitted with drop tanks.

In January 1944 the first raid on an enemy airfield was carried out, dropping 500lb bombs on an airfield in Holland. These dive bombing raids had a variable success rate and were phased out later in the year.

From March 1944 the 355th were to develop the tactic of destroying enemy aircraft on the ground or 'ground strafing', for which they were to become famous as the 'Steeple Morden Strafers'.

For an operation on 5 April 1944 the 355th were awarded a Citation for Extraordinary Heroism and Outstanding Performance in destroying fifty one enemy aircraft (forty three on the ground) and eighty one heavily damaged in an operation carried out in exceptionally adverse weather conditions.

On 6 June 1944 (D Day) seventy eight Mustangs from Steeple Morden took off to support the Allied invasion of France. In the days following they carried out bombing and strafing missions over France and also destroyed enemy aircraft in the air.

During 1944 Steeple Morden was home to the 'Scouting Force' – a fast fighter force scouting ahead of a bombing mission to report back accurate and up to date weather conditions to the bombers.

On a lighter note, in June 1944 a concrete tennis court was built at the airfield. It was still there in 1992.

All aircraft movements were logged by a Royal Observer Corps unit stationed at Slip End, Ashwell.

In September 1944 the 355th flew in support of 'Operation Market Garden' over Nijmegen and Arnhem. In the same month, seventy two Mustangs from Steeple Morden escorted bombers dropping supplies to Polish forces in Warsaw.

In December 1944 the Group undertook missions escorting bombers over Germany.

In the early months of 1945 the 355th continued to support bombing operations and destroying enemy aircraft on the ground. For example on 16 April 62 Mustangs strafed three airfields with seventy enemy aircraft destroyed. By the end of April, the Luftwaffe was finished.

With the war over the 355th moved out of Steeple Morden to take on a new role as part of the Army of Occupation in Germany. In all they had flown seventeen thousand sorties and destroyed over five hundred enemy aircraft on the ground and over three hundred and fifty in the air.

The airfield was handed back to the RAF in November 1945 and closed the following September. The runways were removed for use as foundations for the M1 motorway.

Bassingbourn Airfield
Construction
First constructed as a grass airfield with four large hangars, it was not until August of 1941 that three runways and hard-standing areas were built and in April 1942 that the No.1 runway (East-West) was completed.

RAF
In April 1940, 11 OTU (Operational Training Unit) were formed, operating with Wellingtons and Ansons. The airfield came under attack on numerous occasions and there were frequent flying accidents until they left in August 1941.

On 13 August 1941 Ju88s bombed Bassingbourn with devastating results – there were twenty two casualties of which ten were fatal, when a barrack block was hit.

11 OTU participated in the '1,000 bomber raids' in May/June 1942 (see Steeple Morden notes).

USAAF

In October 1942 an initial complement of B-17Fs arrived as part of 91st Bombardment Group (Heavy), 8th Air Force and they were to stay until June 1945. They were known as 'The Ragged Irregulars' during their stay in England. The B-17 Flying Fortress was perhaps the most well known American heavy bomber of the Second World War. The B-17 had four engines and carried a ten man crew. It dropped more bombs than any other U.S. aircraft of the Second World War. Over twelve thousand were built, the first production B-17B was delivered to the USAF in March 1939. Following the end of the war the B-17 was rapidly withdrawn from service, being replaced by the B-29 Superfortress.

Their first mission, in November 1942 was to destroy U-boat installations at Brest. For the next six months they participated in high altitude daylight precision bombing raids. By the end of 1943 three of the original four squadron commanders had been lost. During the first half of 1943 a colour documentary about the 8th Air Force operations was filmed, featuring the 'Memphis Belle' and her crew, the first 91st Group crew to complete a twenty five mission tour. The Memphis Belle was used to tour US airfields to raise money for the war effort.

By January 1944 the Group had flown one hundred missions and six months later they had reached the two hundred mission mark.

With the arrival of long range P-51B Mustangs, the bombers were escorted all the way to their targets, but there were still heavy losses, e.g. on 20 July eight B-17s were lost on a mission to Leipzig and fifteen failed to return on 2 November.

On D-Day continuous raids were mounted on enemy defences in Normandy. By the end of the war the 91st gunners had the highest total of claims for enemy aircraft with four hundred and two destroyed but they also suffered the highest losses of any 8th Air Force Group with one hundred and ninety seven aircraft missing in action.

Post War

After the war the 91st returned to the USA. In July 1945 the station was handed back to RAF Transport Command. The station was involved in training RAF crews and the ferrying of VIPs. There was also considerable involvement in the Berlin Airlift in 1948/49.

In October 1950 the airfield transferred to Bomber Command and there was again an American contingent at Bassingbourn. From September 1951 the first jet bomber training unit in the RAF was set up at Bassingbourn and they were to remain until 1969. For most of this time training was with Canberra bombers.

In late 1969 the airfield was handed over to the Army.

Chapter 15

The Nation and the Village Recover

The Second World War ended on 2 September 1945 with the surrender of Japan although the war in Europe had finished on 8 May 1945. There followed a period of peace until the Korean War started in 1950. From about 1947 a period of tension, both political and military, existed between the Eastern and Western Blocs which became known as the Cold War.

After the Second World War ended the remainder of the 1940's marked a period of reconstruction and recovery which continued into the 1950's. Internationally, new organisations were established to coordinate relationships and dealings between countries. On a national level the UK had to recover financially and rebuild its war torn cities and infrastructure, redeploy its military personnel back into civilian life and address the many social changes which were the result of six years of war. These national imperatives were reflected at a local level in our own village.

International Recovery

Perhaps the most significant event was the founding of the United Nations on 24 October 1945 replacing the ineffective League of Nations. There were fifty one member states initially, now increased to one hundred and ninety three. The U.N. Security Council is charged with the maintenance of international peace and security and Britain is a permanent member of this body.

The World Bank and International Monetary Fund were created in 1944. These bodies aim to reduce poverty around the world. The World Bank provides loans to developing countries and the IMF works to improve the economies of its member states.

Unesco and Unicef were established towards the end of 1946. Unesco aims to foster peace by moral and intellectual solidarity e.g. through education. Unicef protects children around the world by addressing disease, hunger, conflict and violence.

In December 1948 the United Nations adopted the Universal Declaration of Human Rights. This was the first expression of the rights to which all human beings are entitled.

The North Atlantic Treaty Organisation (NATO) was established in April 1949, as a mutual defence pact between the USA and its European member states.

On a lighter note, international sporting activities gradually returned to normal after the war years. The 1948 Olympic Games were held in London but they were known as the Austerity Games because of the economic climate and rationing. This was the first Summer Olympics since the 1936 Games in Berlin. Germany and Japan were not allowed to participate and the USSR declined to attend. A record fifty nine nations were represented by over four thousand athletes in nineteen sporting disciplines.

The United Kingdom

By the end of the war this country was exhausted and economically 'on its knees'. Industry had to be redirected from supporting the needs of a nation at war to peacetime recovery. In the eighteen months from June 1945 over four million men and women returned to 'civvy street'. Since 1940 the country had been led by a coalition government under Churchill, but this broke up in May 1945. A General Election was held in July 1945 and a Labour Government under Clement Attlee was returned. Their campaign promised to create full employment, a universal National Health Service and a 'cradle to grave' welfare state. These policies were based on the Beveridge Report of 1942, which sought to address poverty, poor education, inadequate medical services, homelessness, poor housing and unemployment. The Labour Party continued in office until 1951, having introduced the National Health Service in 1948; sickness and unemployment benefits; improved retirement pensions and more council housing. 20% of the economy was nationalised.

The economy was also greatly aided by the Marshall Plan. This was implemented in 1948 and continued for four years. The United States provided economic support to help rebuild the economies of Western Europe. The UK received over a quarter of the funds provided. This helped to rebuild damaged infrastructure and modernise industry.

However, after winning the war, many felt that life should have been better than it was, drab and impoverished, with the continuation and intensification of rationing. For example the meat ration was reduced and potatoes were rationed. The country then suffered in 1947 one of the worst winters in living memory. Millions of workers were idle due to power cuts to industry and many areas were snow covered for the whole of February. The Prime Minister could offer no better news - *"I have no easy words for the nation. I cannot say when we will emerge into easier times."*

The country was however lifted from the gloom by the wedding of Princess Elizabeth and Philip Mountbatten in November 1947.

Our village

The situation in Guilden Morden was generally no better than in the country as a whole. After the war, there was a gradual return to normality. Living conditions slowly improved. The mains water supply and mains electricity had already reached the village and these were gradually extended to all areas and were connected within each house to improve daily life. However, electrical appliances such as refrigerators and washing machines, that we take for granted today, were still not within reach of most households and of course televisions were a rarity until the 1950's. As mentioned above rationing continued into the 1950's but the impact on people living in the country was less than for those in the towns.

However, the departure of American servicemen from the area would have reduced the supply of sweets and some other treats.

Plans were in place for some additional Council housing but there were still no Council refuse collections and requests for street lighting had not been agreed. Conditions at the village school were still inadequate according to Parish Council minutes of 1947, although the older children could now complete their (secondary) education at Bassingbourn School.

The closure of the Steeple Morden air base in 1946 had a significant impact on the surrounding villages. The skies were quieter and there were no longer service personnel around who had provided a boost to the local pubs and shops in the area. RAF Bassingbourn continued, of course, but without the American presence.

It was still the case that few people owned cars and petrol was available only for essential motoring. Foreign holidays were banned. The bus services to the village were better than today, but were still inadequate, according to Parish Council minutes. Residents continued to stay mainly in the village for shopping and recreation. The village bakery, blacksmith, Post Office and Annie Murfitt's shop continued into the 1950's as did the six pubs. Village sporting activity returned as the recreation ground became available for football, cricket and tennis.

There were major changes to employment in the area as war time production in factories in the local towns ceased and were replaced in time with other manufacturing enterprises. Those returning from military service were usually able to find work in the towns or on the farms, which still employed more workers than today, until mechanisation was fully introduced.

And so, change came to the village gradually in the post war 1940's, with life returning to normal and standards of living slowly improving. It would not be until the 1950's that the pace of change would increase.

Appendix 1

Airman's Letters

The following letters are fictitious. They describe the feelings of a United States airman serving in Steeple Morden when writing home to his family. They were written for us by Mrs Jean Warren who has lived in both the USA and England.

Arriving

Dear Mom   October 1943

This is just a short letter to let you know we've arrived safely and you can stop worrying about the accommodation. We're warm and comfortable and we've struck real lucky with a camp near a quaint little village that's just like we imagined it. The guys who've been here since July say there are houses (cottages they call them) that are more than a hundred years old and they've got those thatched roofs like we see in all the pictures. There's an old stone church that must be at least five hundred years old and Joe and I intend to go to service there on Sunday if we're allowed off-base. We want to see what it looks like inside.

Several of the new guys are planning to go into the village for a look as soon as we get the opportunity. It's not that far away and we've all been issued with bicycles to go about on as we can't use the jeeps because of petrol shortages (it took us a while to work out they meant gas.) They're not at all like American bikes; the brakes are on the handlebars instead of the pedals and I've acquired a few cuts and bruises when I've forgotten that. Apparently Oswald Kaye, the blacksmith, is making a fortune running a cycle repair shop as a sideline. He's certainly getting a lot of trade from us. Most of the guys reckon that flying a 'Jug' (P-47 Thunderbolt) is much safer. We've seen a few horse riders around as well, though not like in Texas. They don't look that comfortable on a horse and they only manage a gentle walk along the lanes (that's roads to us, though they're so narrow I wouldn't want to, see anyone coming in the other direction.)

They don't number the streets here like we do at home either. They've all got names, like Church Street and Hay Street and Trap Road. The captain told us at the familiarization briefing that the names come from the old days when people couldn't read and so had to navigate by the things they could see from the road. We'll probably have to do the same because there aren't any maps available, and even if there were we couldn't use them after dark because we can't use flashlights (they call them torches) in case the Germans see the light from the air. Not that there have been any bombs around here, so you needn't worry about that either, Mom. The worst thing is the weather and we're learning how to fly through fog. I can understand why the locals call it pea soup - it's thick, green and dirty looking and impossible to see through. There have been a few close encounters with the hill at the end of one runway but I think we've all got it worked out now.

Your loving son,

Jeff

Pubs

Hey Dad,   2ⁿᵈ November 1943

We've been here a few weeks now and we're getting to know the local community and trying to fit in. We cycle to the village regularly and most of us remember to stay on the left, though we sometimes get a bit confused on the way back from the pub.

For a small village this place has an incredible number of pubs and one of the guys challenged Joe and me to drink some of the local ale in all of them last night. Apparently there's a brewery in the next village that supplies all the pubs for miles around with the warm, flat stuff they call beer around here. At first we thought the lack of ice was another wartime restriction but Bertie Steele, the landlord at the Edward VII, tells us they always drink it like that. "Why would you want cold beer?" he says. Well, maybe he's got a point in this climate. If the wind isn't threatening to blow us off our bikes then the rain's attempting to wash us off.

Well, Bertie relieved us of 2s 6d for the disgusting stuff (you wouldn't believe how complicated the money is here) and we were still reasonably sober when we left the Edward. By the way, I don't know whether I should have mentioned the name, but there must be hundreds of Edward VII's all over England and the censor can scrub it out if he doesn't like it. All the pubs here have very strange names. Bertie says they're mostly named after kings or the pictures they had on their shields to tell everyone what side they were on in a war. Well, there should certainly be a few new names around after this war then. 'The Union Jack' or 'The Stars and Stripes' might be a bit disrespectful, but what about 'The British Bulldog' or 'Government Issue'.

Anyway, the next on our list was the Pear Tree in what they call New Road, though to me it looked just as old as everywhere else around here. The locals all seemed to be playing darts (you remember that game we read about in the familiarization instructions) and they invited us to join in. They were kind enough to say my aim was pretty good for a beginner, but after one of them had bought a round and Joe and I both felt obliged to do the same I didn't seem able to hit the target any more and Joe thought it might be a good idea to move on.

I don't think we got through all the pubs but I do remember we finished at the Green Man. That's where the landlord told us there are laws about being drunk in charge of a bicycle here and made us walk back to base. He's locked the bikes in his shed and we have to go back for them at opening time. Tell Mom I'll come straight back though and I'll push the bike. I might fall off if I try to ride it and I surely won't remember to stay on the left. This British beer's a real killer!

Your slightly befuddled son,

Jeff

Dance

Dear Sis,   3ʳᵈ February 1944

Congratulations! Send a snap as soon as you can, please. I will have to get to know my niece at second hand until I get leave and can come home to meet her in the flesh. There's very little here I can send as a Christening present (there's a war on, as they keep telling us) but I enclose a pressed English rose for her. They grow in great profusion here, I'm told, and always look fresh and beautiful, not tired and drooping like in our Texas gardens. Doubtless it's due to the not so beautiful English rain!

While I'm on the subject of English roses I have to tell you I've met some very pretty girls while I've been here. You would probably say they don't make the best of themselves because they dress very plainly, but that's because clothes are rationed and so they have to 'make do and mend.' I don't know much about female fashion but I can see there's not a lot of material in their skirts. They're very straight, not flowing like yours, and when they want to look smart they paint their legs with tea and draw a line up the back because they haven't any stockings. The guys who have been here a while know that stockings are the best present you can give a girl. Make-up is scarce too, but all the girls seem to have soft, white skin so I don't think it matters that they can't powder it. Joe says they paint their lips with blackberry juice. He knows because he's tasted it. Send me some stockings, please, and then I might get the chance to taste it too.

They held a dance in the village hall last week and invited us all to attend. The food was plain country fare but good, but in every other way the scarcity of resources was very evident. There was a limited supply of records and none of the latest hits, and they didn't know how to jitterbug or do any of the latest dances. The thing I really noticed though was how the American men outnumbered the British ones. Although farm workers are excused the draft many of the younger men have gone anyway and a lot the work is being done by the women. Some of them are land girls, sent out from the town to farm the land in the absence of the men. Most of those I danced with told me they have husbands or brothers fighting overseas and some even have sisters serving in the women's army or air-force. It made me realize how easy we have it at home compared to the British. They've long since abandoned the concept of 'the little woman at home.' Now they do everything a working man should do. I'm told some even hold commissions and if they give a man an order then he has to jump to. I can't imagine how that would go down in our army.

I felt very humble at that dance, I can tell you. These British women don't have much but they're determined to make the best of what they've got and seize all the enjoyment they can get. The very least they deserve is a new pair of stockings, so send some please to the newly created uncle and your loving brother,

Jeff

Evacuees

Dear Susie,   4th April 1944

Thank you for the nice letter you sent me and I'm glad to hear that Sam is helping you with your spelling now that I'm gone.

As you're studying about England at school I thought you might like to hear something about English children for your class project. There are an awful lot of children in this village and many of them are evacuees (you might have to ask Sam to help with that word.) It means they are children who have been sent away from London because it's too dangerous for them to live there. Their parents tie a label round their necks with their name on it and send them off on the train to live with families in the countryside where it's safe. Can you imagine that? They don't know anything about the people they are going to live with. They just arrive at the station and someone sorts them out and allocates them to a family. Everyone who has a guest room, or even a spare bed, has to take in children, and most of them are poor, skinny little things, because there's not much food in London either.

The kids are all very scared when they first arrive but fortunately most families are good to them and soon feed them up and make them feel welcome. Most of the houses are very overcrowded but nobody complains too much. They call it doing their bit for the war effort and try to treat the evacuees the same as their own kids.

There are two brothers here, one black and one white, and they stay in different homes but spend most of the day together. Marriage between black and white is allowed here. Some of our guys don't like to see that and try to cause trouble but the English won't stand for it and I think they're right. Joseph and Adam are great kids and we can't claim to be fighting for freedom if we won't stand up for a child because his skin is the wrong color. Don't you let anyone tell you different about that, Susie.

The school is too small to cope with all these extra children so most of the evacuees have to have their lessons in the village hall. They've had to bring in extra teachers as well and they all add to the overcrowding. It doesn't feel like there's much space over here, but then I suppose the whole country is smaller than Texas and there are a lot more people in it.

British children don't get much candy, which they call sweets, because there's not enough sugar to make it, so I give the kids my Hershey bars whenever I've got some. It reminds me of you when I see them with chocolate all over their faces and I'm glad you're safe over there with Mom and Dad and not having to be an evacuee.

Give my love to all the family and give yourself a big hug from your loving brother,

Jeff

Games

Hi Sam,   5th July 1944

You'd be amazed to see what a proper English gentleman your brother is becoming. The British are so polite they would never comment when we do or say the wrong thing but, in the nicest possible way, they manage to make us feel like real hicks from the backwoods. We're learning to recognize that a raised eyebrow means we're out of order, and we see it quite a lot when we say 'bloody' in mixed company or don't wait our turn for something.

A few weeks ago Joe and I went to watch the local football team playing against a team from the next village. They were mostly teenagers, likely to be called up in the next few months I would think, and any half-decent American team could have run rings round them. Anyway, Joe and I were shouting all the usual things, like "missed by a mile" and "take him off," and we suddenly noticed everyone else had gone quiet. Then somebody shouted "good try", though it was anything but, and everyone else applauded. We'd clearly done it again! Though nobody said anything it was obviously "not the done thing" to insult the players, and after that we applauded every missed goal and didn't cheer too loudly when our side won. That's bad form as well!

Our bad manners have clearly been forgiven though, because yesterday those same teenagers invited us to take a turn with the cricket bat. They tried to explain the rules, but I don't think we were any wiser at the end than at the beginning. I'm glad I didn't say that hitting a ball with such a large bat would be a piece of cake for a baseball player because it's a completely different technique and surprisingly difficult to do. I was bowled out twice before I even managed to hit the ball and Joe didn't do much better. However, once we got the hang of it we were invited to play one on each team, and if we didn't exactly distinguish ourselves as batsmen we at least put in a reasonable performance as fielders.

After the practice we were invited for cheese sandwiches and lemonade in the village hall, most players being too young to drink alcohol. Everyone complimented us on the catches we made and nobody mentioned out terrible batting. I can't imagine any American crowd behaving like that, but there's something to be said for it. It makes for an enjoyable match, however badly the game is played, and it seemed a good way to celebrate Independence Day in a spirit of friendship with the old country.

Tell Mom she won't recognize her well-mannered son when he returns but I hope she'll be proud of the man I'm becoming.

Your gentlemanly, cricket-playing brother,

Jeff

London

Dear Sis,   6th October 1944

Joe and I got a few days leave last week and decided to spend it in London. We went there in the smallest, grimiest train you can imagine, with no restaurant car or bell-boys, and it stopped at dozens of grubby little stations along the way. We talked with some of the passengers who got on and off and they said it wasn't like that before the war; there's just no-one left to do all the maintenance jobs now.

London is like nothing I've ever seen before and I don't know how to begin describing it. It's a dirty and devastated city full of tired people in shabby clothes, but for all that there's an air of frantic gaiety about it - everyone making the most of what might be their last day, I guess. In the evening the theatres and cinemas carry on despite the air raid sirens, and then hundreds of people leave to sleep on subway platforms because their homes have disappeared. In the morning they line up to wash in public bath-houses and walk to work through piles of rubble as if there were nothing unusual about the situation. And amidst all this stand the most wonderful buildings I've ever seen. The jewel of them all is St. Paul's Cathedral, a mere three hundred years old to the British but ancient history to me and Joe and the most beautiful building we've ever seen. I can understand why Londoners feel the way they do about it. We're proud of having the biggest buildings in the world but the British value the age of theirs. The Tower of London is nearly a thousand years old and full of very bloody history. Hundreds of people were imprisoned, tortured and beheaded there, including a few of King Henry VIII's wives. Parts of the Houses of Parliament are just as old, though new bits have been added all through the centuries. William the Conqueror was crowned there in 1066 but Big Ben is less than a hundred years old - a mere baby to the British, despite its size. I've bought postcards of them all to show you when I get home.

We headed for Hyde Park expecting wide open spaces and beautiful flower gardens but it's been turned into a mammoth vegetable plot, along with all the other parks in London. I suspect most of what's grown goes to feed the people lining up at the soup kitchens. Nobody seems to feel any shame at using these places; hunger, homelessness and worn out clothes are almost a mark of pride because they make people understand what 'the boys over there' are going through. Thankfully we boys over here have a warm, comfortable base to go back to. I don't think I'm cut out for London life as it is at the moment.

Keep my little niece warm and safe and give her a kiss from me.

Jeff

Death

Dear Mom,   7th April 1945

There is no easy way to write this. Joe died today. I don't know whether you will get this letter before the official telegram comes, or even what it will say, but I wish you will go to see his mom and tell her it was very quick and he didn't suffer. I wouldn't lie to her about that. It was a daytime raid and I saw his plane blown to bits in the sky above the English Channel. He probably didn't even see the enemy who fired on him from behind. If my time has to come I hope it will be like that.

Now I have begun to understand the meaning of war in a personal way. In this quiet little village the people wouldn't even know there was a war on if it weren't for the rationing - and two thousand Americans of course! There's a lot of aircraft noise and a bomb did fall on a local farm a few weeks ago and shattered a greenhouse, but that's about all it did. For the rest, life goes on for the locals pretty much as usual. They do notice those of us who don't come back after each mission but they don't know us well enough to grieve. It would be a lonely death we die here had we not become like family to each other, but we have grown beyond the pain of each loss. There have been too many and there is a limit to the tears one can cry, even for one's best friend.

I want you to tell his mom about the last day we spent together. It was the best time we have had in England and I shall remember it as long as I live. It was a fine spring day with flowers in bloom everywhere and we rode the bus to the local town along with the women going to work in the factories. These English buses are quite something - old and battered and low-powered, but you should see how far they can go on how little gas. It was so crowded it seemed like all those packed onto the step at the back must fall off but we all managed to cling on and got there slowly but safely.

Joe and I wandered round old churches, bought souvenirs in old shops, chatted to pretty girls in the park and had afternoon tea in a quaint old teashop. (That's a very civilized custom and I'm getting to like it a lot.) In the evening we saw "Casablanca" at the cinema and almost missed the last bus back to base because we had to stand at attention for the national anthem. It's quite acceptable to rush out before it starts but everyone stops just where they are when the first note sounds, even if they're almost out of the door.

I'm glad Joe had that as his last experience of this country. I'm glad I have it as my last memory of him. Please tell his mother so from me.

Your loving and grieving son,

Jeff

VE Day

Dear Sam,   8th May 1945

Great celebrations! Victory is won in Europe and the Great British reserve has entirely vanished. People are hugging and kissing in the streets, church bells are ringing and there are bonfires on the village green that will light the night sky long after the blackout curtains should be closed. It's a transformed world, and I feel as overwhelmed by it as I did on my first day here. At the base there's a strange mixture of emotions: relief that it's over for us here but also the knowledge that America's war in the east goes on; the expectation of going home and the knowledge of friends who must be left behind. I don't think any of us really know what we feel, other than a great relief that there are no more missions to be flown. No doubt there will be celebrations in the mess tonight but I think I might prefer to go and drink warm beer in a village pub. It's a British celebration rather than ours and it will be good to share it with the friends we've made here.

I was in Annie Murfitt's shop this morning attempting to buy celebratory candy for the kids and all the talk was of the things that might be available again soon. I've grown used to the way things are here but I looked again at the gaps on the shelves and remembered my first impressions, colored no doubt by the history we learned at school. Back then I thought this was a worn-out country, governed by an outmoded class system and destined for the scrap heap of history, and my first experience of cold trains, dirty stations and unpainted houses confirmed that view. Now I know differently. The British are a tough people, prepared to do what it takes and suffer what they must. People are cold because all the power goes to the armaments factories, houses are unpainted because people have more important things to do and shelves are empty because the food goes to the troops and the children. I should like to see what it will look like here in another five years when all that effort has been diverted to rebuilding and restoring what must once have been. I should like to see what the women look like when they have stockings and pretty dresses and make-up on their faces. I should like to see what a true family looks like, with all its members present in a brightly painted cottage with roses at the door. It's the sort of romanticism you'd scoff at, I suppose, but it makes a pretty picture after the grey uniformity of war.

I do not know what our orders will be now. My draft papers say I must serve for six months after the end of the war but it won't be over until the Japanese surrender. Everyone says that won't be long now so I hope everyone is right. Some of us will be going to Germany or Japan but if I'm lucky perhaps I'll get to serve my time out here - and if you're lucky everything will be over before your draft papers come.

Happy Birthday, little brother! What a wonderful week to turn eighteen!

Jeff

Going Home

Dear Dad,   9th July 1945

No doubt you have seen the pictures of Belsen as we have over here. It is a terrible thing to say but in some ways I was glad to see such dreadful sights, because now I know there was a good reason for what we have done ourselves. There's no glory in war but perhaps, after all, there is some honor in duty done and civilized values upheld, however uncivilized the manner of that upholding.

This is a very somber letter but I can no longer write light-heartedly about dances and cricket matches and English roses. The men are beginning to return here and it is not as it should be. Some of them are wounded in their bodies but all are wounded in their minds and, worse still, they seem like strangers to the wives. Domestic harmony does not return overnight, and I think in many cases it never will. I have felt what is in the mind of those men, though I have not seen it as closely as they have, and it is not something that can be shared with those who were not there. And yet what is marriage without sharing? The women, too, are not what they were five years ago. They are independent creatures, used to ruling their own lives, and they will not surrender that independence easily. Rough times lie ahead in many households I fear.

It is the same for us. Dear Dad, I think you will not know the son who returns to you soon. I am no longer the boy who left you two years ago, nor am I the man I might have become in better, happier times. I have lost so many of those who shared my life here and I wonder if I will have any place amongst you all who have not seen the things I have seen or done the things I have done. I think often of Houseman's land of lost contentment and fear I never will come there again.

My god seems very distant from me now and I cling fast instead to the memory of family and friends. I long to be with you all in that dry, dusty place I call home, and the humble son of a quiet, small-town schoolmaster seems just about the best thing in the world to be right now. Texas may not be as pretty as this country but it is where I hope my bruised and battered soul might find some peace again.

This will be the last letter you receive before you see me again, but kill no fatted calf and celebrate but quietly among yourselves. Your son is one of the few who are coming home.

Jeff

Appendix 2

Guilden Morden Townlands Trust Charity

Charities for the Poor

The origins of the charities for the poor first appeared in 1635 when a certain John Godfrey left £10, the interest to be given to the poor at Christmas and Whitsun. The parish borrowed this £10 and two other bequests in 1662 to pay for church repairs, undertaking to pay the interest to the poor. This arrangement continued until around 1720. In 1843 it was learnt that arrears of £70 were due and the vestry decided to give £4 yearly in coal at Christmas. This seems to have been absorbed into the town lands charity in the 1880's.

After 1806 it was decided to use the yield of the town lands for relief of the needy after allowing £12 yearly for church repairs. The income in the 1820's was £55. Around 1830 the parish temporarily exchanged its 45 acre holding for 35 acres nearer the village, let as allotments to forty three labourers.

In 1842 the then vicar of Guilden Morden made a copy of the ancient town book of Guilden Morden which was commenced in 1662 soon after the Restoration of King Charles II. This showed that the money left for the poor of the parish had in fact been appropriated by the church authorities to repair the church. It had been in the hands of the churchwardens but the constable took over and paid out the poor relief at the rate of 6% or at such rate as 'ye law of the land shall allow for money', this to be paid at Christmas and Easter.

These arrangements ended in 1857 when, after complaints by the vicar, the town land rent, £86 altogether, was divided equally between the poor and church repairs. Until the 1870's the trust was in the hands of an autocratic churchwarden who allegedly gave over a third of the poor's share to non-residents. From 1898 the parish council managed their half share as a separate charity and until the 1950's its income was commonly given in small cash doles, three hundred and sixty eight people sharing £32 4s. in 1896. In the mid 1960's the poor's £51 went mostly in doles to thirty five people. By the 1970's £90-£100 was given yearly among thirty five to forty elderly people.

This relief is paid to this day from money collected from land income and is known as the Guilden Morden Townlands Charity, the umbrella under which the Trustees of the Poors and Church Charities jointly administer the land, collect revenue and divide the proceeds as required by the deed.

Source: Victoria County History - Cambridgeshire - Guilden Morden Parish

Charity Land

Currently (2015) the charity owns four parcels of land for which it receives rent; 8 acres in *Ashwell Parish*, (currently farmed by C Murfitt); 4 acres along *Icknield Way* and 35.5 acres at the *Chalk Pit* (JE Huffer); and 3 acres at the *Gravel Pit* by Highfield Farm, known locally as the Red Barns (PJ & NA Chapman).

It also receives payments through the Countryside Higher Level Stewardship scheme for just over 19 acres of this land, including 8.23 acres of Parish Council land (the Craft), these payments it shares with the Parish Council.

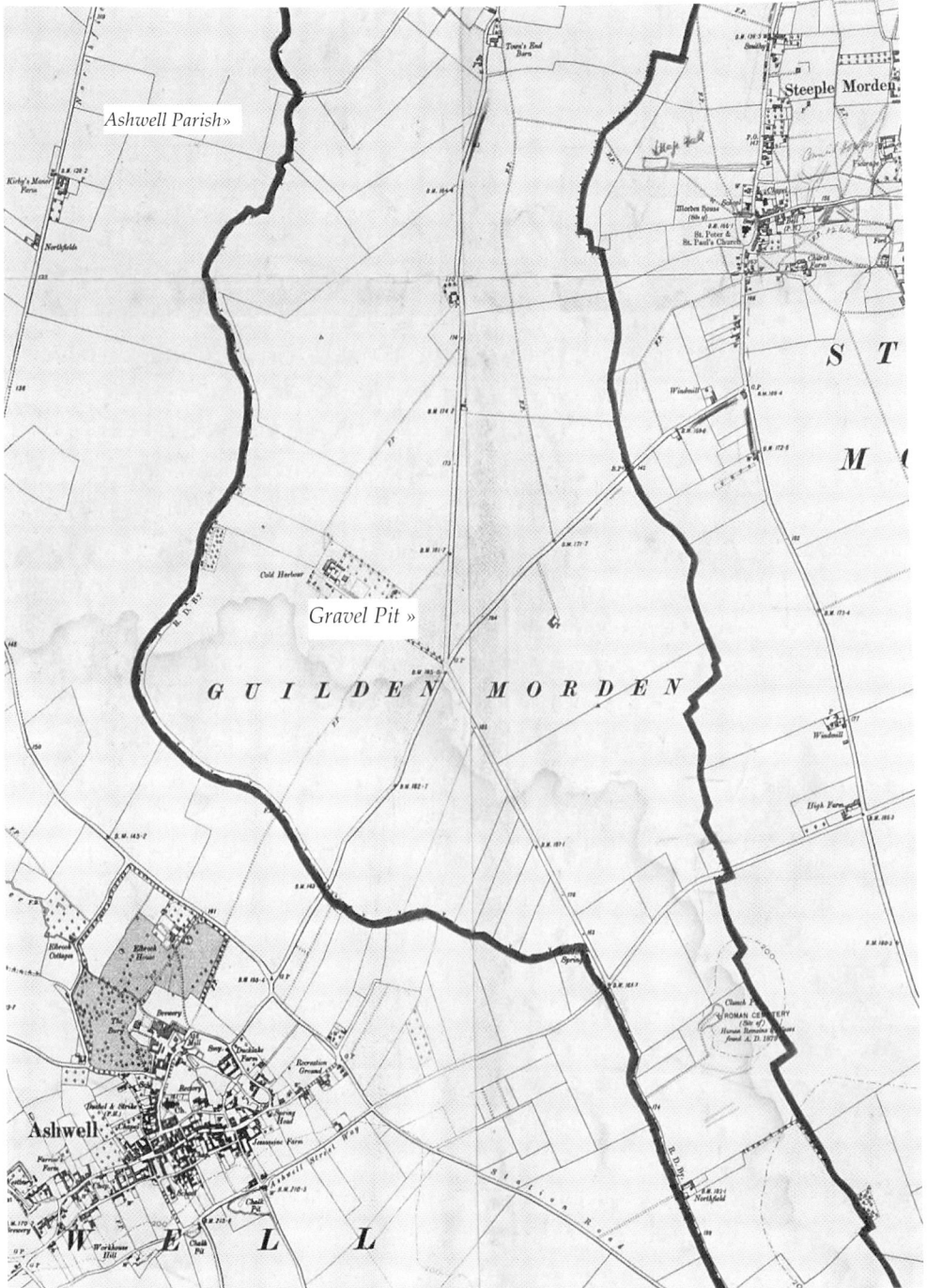

Sealed 1st May 1896.

1329/96.

TEN SHILLINGS

Stamps 10s.

TEN SHILLINGS

County—**CAMBRIDGE.**
Parish—**GUILDEN MORDEN.**
Charity—**Town Lands.**

C.
61,930.

Order for Apportionment and Management under Local Government Act, 1894, s. 75 (2), including—Appointment of Trustees, and Vesting in Official Trustee of Charity Lands.

CHARITY COMMISSION.

In the Matter of the Charity called or known as The TOWN LANDS, in the Parish of GUILDEN MORDEN, in the County of CAMBRIDGE, administered under an Opinion of the Charity Commissioners sealed on the 3rd April 1857;

In the Matter of "The Local Government Act, 1894"; and

In the Matter of "The Charitable Trusts Acts, 1853 to 1894."

The Board of Charity Commissioners for England and Wales, on the application of the Parish Council of the above-mentioned Parish :

And it appearing that the endowment of the above-mentioned Charity is held in part only for purposes of an Ecclesiastical Charity :

Do hereby, in execution of the provisions of section 75 (2) of the Local Government Act, 1894, **Order** as follows :—

1. One half of the yearly income of the property constituting the endowment of the Charity (consisting of the particulars specified in the Schedule hereto, and all other the endowment, if any, of the Charity) is hereby separated from the rest of that endowment, and shall henceforth be the endowment of an Ecclesiastical Charity, to be called the Church Charity :

2. The Vicar and Churchwardens for the time being of the Parish of Guilden Morden are hereby appointed to be the Trustees of the Church Charity :

3. The remainder of the original Charity shall henceforth be called the Poor Charity :

4. The Trustees of the Poor Charity shall consist of four persons to be appointed from time to time by the Parish Council of the said Parish for a term four years in each case, but of the persons first so appointed two, to be determined by lot, shall go out of office at the end of two years from the date of their appointment, but shall be eligible for re-appointment :

5. The aforesaid property (so far as the same is not of copyhold tenure) is hereby vested in "The Official Trustee of Charity Lands," for all the estate and interest therein belonging to or held in trust for the Charities :

6. All of the said property shall be managed jointly by the Trustees of the Church Charity and the Trustees of the Poor Charity.

SCHEDULE OF PROPERTY.

Description.	Extent.			Tenant.	Gross Yearly Income.		
	A.	R.	P.		£	s.	d.
Church Pits Farm	40	0	0	John Hall	40	0	0
Gravel Pits	3	0	0	Twelve Cottagers	4	16	0
Ruddery	4	0	0	Thomas Kerbyshire	6	0	0
Land in Parish of Ashwell	2	0	0	Alfred Long	3	0	0
	2	0	0	Wilfred Rule	3	0	0
	2	0	0	John Parrish	3	0	0
	2	0	0	Thomas Clarke	3	0	0

Sealed by Order of the Board this 1st day of May 1896.

L.S.

AUTHORIZED UNDER 50. & 51. VICT. C. 49. SEC. 3.

Townland Trust Deed 1896
Reproduced by kind permission of the Townlands Trust

Appendix 3

Oral History Recordings

We are grateful to the following, who agreed to subject themselves to the ordeal of speaking in front of the microphone, as part of our series of oral history recordings.

Freda Adlington (nee Williams)
Born 1934 in Church Street, Guilden Morden, eventually moving to Trap Road with her parents Tom and Hilda Williams. She married David Adlington in 1962.

"...... A lot more open spaces. It was a village in those days. I was only saying to Cynthia when we walked down the road, I couldn't believe these were where the old stables were for the big house and everybody was happier I'm sure, more content. I think people were much more... They've got a lot more today and things, but I don't know if there's contentment. And we knew what it was to want things but we didn't used to worry did we? If we hadn't got it, we hadn't got it. We didn't have to say, 'Oh they've got it down the road, and they've not.' But no, the village has really really changed from our day, hasn't it?......"

Marjorie Baker (nee Thompson)
Born 1934 in Cambridge, but her home was 4 Avenel Terrace, Guilden Morden before moving across the road to *Ivy Cottage* with her parents William (the postman) and Marjorie Thompson. She married Peter Baker in 1956.

. *"When I went out to work at 15, I went to my hairdressing apprenticeship, because you used to travel on the bus every day to Hitchin. But I used to sometimes go to the pictures maybe on a Saturday evening, but I had to... it wasn't very often that I done all that, and used to just come home and do whatever I wanted to do, or maybe go out and see my friends or something like that. But I was very restricted on what I could do because the thing was that I always had to be doing something that fitted in whatever the parents thought was right. You know, so I used to go up the rec, we used to go up the rec and play up there a lot and things like that. Or we'd go for a walk, through the fields and everywhere, you know, and go out and about in that way. But there was a Tuesday, this would be after the War I suppose, yeah, the Tuesday night, because I was sort of, yeah, teenager time, and there was the pictures in the Village Hall, I'm not sure if it was Tuesday or Thursday night, but it was not exactly the magic lantern, I don't know what it was. They showed the old George Formby films and cowboys and all that sort of thing, and it was nine pence to go in".*

Brenda Davies (nee Thompson)
Born 1934 in Hitchin, daughter of David and Dorothy Thompson. She lived in Ashwell Road, Guilden Morden with her aunt, as her mother had died two years after she was born. She married William Davis in 1951 in Cambridge.

"...... The school. Well I think it consisted of the infants and juniors, I suppose, and another room. My first teacher I remember was Mrs Munden. I'm not sure. And there was also another teacher that we had come, and her name was... well, her name now is Gwen Melody, which she still happens to be alive, and she's 100 years old, because she celebrated it recently. Mrs Kershaw was the main teacher there, who I think she suddenly disappeared one day. And we were left with no teacher at all...... "

Derek Dellar
Born 1934 in Phoenix Row (Fox Hill Road), Guilden Morden before moving to one of the new Council houses in New Road with his parents Oswald & Naomi Dellar. He married Rita Unwin in 1964.

Interviewer *"Did you have a radio?"*
"......We had one, yeah. In the wartime we used to... well, after the war, cor, great big old thing it was, you know. Well they used to be, didn't they? And the... you had a battery, like a car battery really, and an accumulator, so you had the two. And they used to bring it, or take it to Royston every week... Well, they used to deliver, like charge them up, and leave one, take the other one away. And because they'd charged it up that'd last about a week, you see. But the battery was like that. Great big... And that's how you went on...."

John Dellar
Born 1935 at 'Robin Dell', Guilden Morden son of Harry and Margaret Dellar. He married Una Oyston, daughter of Jack and Winifred Oyston of Ashwell, in 1967.

"..... My father was chapel and my mother was church. I was sent to chapel Sunday School and escorted down the road with my father on his bicycle, I was on a little three wheeled bicycle and I can remember getting to the chapel gates and Mr Bill Gentle and Mr Matthews tried to get me to go inside and I put the brake on and refused. I wouldn't get off my bike. I shouted and screamed apparently and my father who had been hiding in Swan Lane, because he had taken me that far, but no further, decided to come and take me home. And I didn't go to Sunday School then for about three or four months apparently and then suddenly I said I wanted to go to church Sunday School and my father gave me a real lecture and said "If I take you to the gates this time, you will get clouted if you don't go in." Muriel and Jessica were going to church Sunday school and I went with them and went in and I went to church Sunday school until I left school I think......"

Graham Dellar
Born 1935 in Ashwell Road, Guilden Morden son of Jim and
Winifred Dellar. He married Barbara Waldock in 1958 in Ashwell,
Christine Allardyce in 1974 in Cambridge and finally (we hope)
Patricia Saunders in 2005 in Australia.

*".......Well the Home Guard, my father was in the Home Guard. The chap next door, Alf
Sole was the sergeant. And then there was the Fire Brigade. I remember them. The Air Raid
Wardens and I actually remember the Army being posted around the area and there was a
search light at Beverley Farm in Steeple Morden. There was an anti-aircraft gun in
Guilden Morden, just off the Ashwell Road, where the Ashwell Road joins the High Street,
on the little bend there. Just up the footpath there they dug a hole and had an anti-aircraft
gun there for a while. Peter Wiggett remembers that in his memories, that he has written
for our history group......"*

Phyllis Dennis (nee Huffer)
Born 1921 near the Chapel in Pound Green, Guilden Morden daughter of Arthur
and Sarah Huffer. She married Maurice Dennis in 1943 in Guilden Morden.

Interviewer: "What was life like after the war"-
*"Well just normal, we had to carry on the same as usual, we didn't do anything exciting
because we ain't got no money. But I got £2.4s.3d, his army pay and my father was
drawing the pension then. So I used to sign it and he used to get that money, and every
week he would put the £2 in the Post Office Savings Bank and brought me the 4s.3d home".*

Barbara Haines (nee Leonard)
Born 1934 in 'Phoenix Row' (Fox Hill Road), Guilden Morden
daughter of Vic and Winifred Leonard. She married Brian Haines in
1959 in Guilden Morden.

*"......I remember leaving Guilden Morden school and going to Bassingbourn, and we used
to have to go on Gentle's coaches and it would go to Wrestlingworth crossroads, along to
Tadlow, the edge of Croydon, then to Wendy, Shingay, North End Bassingbourn down to
the Bassingbourn old school. The headmaster there was Mr Harcourt, and we enjoyed
going to Bassingbourn, it was something different for us. I loved the cooking, but the
sewing. I didn't like. And I have a school report actually of Bassingbourn and cooking has
got a good mark, sewing has 'I could have done better'. But I still don't like sewing, so that
comes with age I am afraid......"*

Don Mackarsie
Born 1930 in East Ham, London, moving to Guilden Morden as a private evacuee in 1940 with his mother Violet, who helped to care for the evacuees in Morden House. He married Peggy Moss of Beverley Farm in 1957.

".......Yes, it was still operational but had tapered off quite a bit. I mean they no longer had the milk round and that sort of thing. But Mr Thompson was still producing Jersey milk by then, which he was selling wholesale. And then shortly after I left he packed up as well. And he went over to like beef cattle more. And just to keep the meadows in order. And I was still working with him, we still worked together. And then he retired in about 1985 '86, and went to Norfolk. And when John Boston took over up here, that's when I then took over all the meadows and I was running them for myself then......"

Doreen Mitchell (nee Izzard)
Born 1934 in *'Avenel Terrace'*, Guilden Morden, daughter of Cyril and Emily Izzard. She married Roy Mitchell in Cambridge in 1954.

"...and my grandmother lived across the road, and I can remember her...she used to wear long dresses and an apron. And when the harvest was around we used to go with her every year and pick up ears of corn, so that we could feed the chickens for the rest of the year, so that we got eggs and things like that. Also Gran always used to have a pig. She'd got a large open chimney, with a copper one side and a little oven the other side. And up this huge chimney there was a pig used to hang, a whole pig. And they used to smoke it. Then we'd always got some bacon. That is one thing I know my grandmother used to do".

Marie Parker (nee Huffer)
Born 1932 in Ashwell Road, Guilden Morden, daughter of Cecil & Elsie Huffer. She married Dennis Parker in 1953 in Guilden Morden.

".......We used to have Mr Price come once a week and give us education in the bible and that sort of thing. The vicar, yes. Old Digger Price, we used to call him [laughs]. He came once a week to do that. He was quite funny at times, yes. I can't remember much more about the teacher that... Oh, there was a Miss Williams when I first left school. I left at... when I left the village school at fourteen I remember she took about six of us up to London Zoo for a treat. I think there was Diana Tomlin, Betty Evans... John Bowen. And Jack... did I say Jack Waldock? And of course then I left that school and I sat a scholarship to go the Technical College in Cambridge, where I learnt to do shorthand and typing......"

Muriel Ward (nee Dellar)
Born 1930 in the High Street, Guilden Morden daughter of Bill and
Ivy Dellar. She married Fred Ward in 1951 in Guilden Morden.

*"......Yes. We had a huge land mine fall down Trap Road in the fields between Steeple and
Guilden Morden. And that made a crater which was there for many years, even with a tree
growing in it. And we were also bombed down Rectory Farm. The... My mother's sisters
came from Boreham Woods in Chelmsford, to stay with us for a few nights to get some
sleep. And that was the time when Guilden Morden was bombed. Had incendiary bombs
and things, which was... we thought was quite funny. They came here for peace and quiet
and we had... I remember the doodlebug going over, which crashed down... memory's bad...
Mobbs Hole, yes, it crashed down Mobbs Hole..."*

Albert Willmott
Born 1924 in Odsey son of Walter and Isabel Willmott. He married Lily Atherton
(below) in 1947 in Steeple Morden.

*"......Well, I started work in the bottling department. They used to have all girls or women
and Mr Fordham had an idea we have boys, so there was the four of us started it down
there. And I don't think that was very successful, I think we messed about too much. And
after the war started, of course, some of the chaps got called up and had to be replaced and
I, so I sat in the office, in the dispatch department getting all the orders from the pubs and
that. The men were allowed quite a few pints actually. You used to come and start at seven
and they'd have a break for breakfast, and they'd have a pint or two
before breakfast some of them...."*

Lily Willmott (nee Atherton)
Born 1926 in Eccles, Manchester. She married Albert Willmott (above) in 1947.

*"......Gradually all my friends kept going in the forces and this friend of mine Irene, we were
the only two really left out of our group. We said we are going to join up, so we went into
town to join up and they said "How old are you?" We said "seventeen". "Oh no you
can't... the only thing you can do is go in the Women's Land Army". So I went home and
my father said "Well that's quite a good idea", because we were being bombed in
Manchester at the time. I used to get on the tram to go to work and if the air raid siren
went we had to get off and go to the nearest air raid shelter, until the all clear went and
then get back on the tram and go into work. So my father said "Well it is quite a good idea
to go into the country". I had been voluntary farming. Our youth clubs were all asked to go
and help farmers to get the harvest in and I found out I quite liked it being out in the open.
So we applied and I said "anything, I will do anything in the Land Army, but I don't want
to be with animals", so when my papers came through I was a diary maid. But I took to it
like a duck takes to water. I loved the cows. I loved the horses. I met Albert at a whist drive
and that was it and we wrote letters every day. We did all our courtship through the post
[laughs] except for on leave......"*

Cynthia Worboys (nee Peckett)
Born 1934 in the Ashwell Road, Guilden Morden daughter of Joe and Priscilla Peckett. She married Maurice Worboys in 1959 in Cambridge.

"......We had Sunday school and first of all it was the Prices... We had it in the vicarage and then we used to... once a month we used to go into church. Then when the Prices moved on we had the Gardiners and it was Mr Gardiner and his sister, who was a deaconess and she took it and she was a lovely little person. She really was. She really made impressions on us. She was very nice. But no we always had Sunday school parties and we used to have Sunday school outings, we used to get bus loads. There used to be about two or three bus loads go to the seaside every year......"

Appendix 4

Village Walks and Other Items of Interest

Village Streets and Buildings
Changes in the village, comparing the present day to the 1940's, were noted during 'village walks' undertaken by the Guilden Morden Local History Group in 2013. Notes produced at the time including the names of some 1940's residents are detailed below.

Pound Green
The building of the Congregational Chapel was started in 1838 and the opening ceremony took place in 1840. The Chapel Minister throughout the 1940's was the Reverend H.F. Hawkes.

Opposite the chapel stands 'Homedale', a Grade II listed building dating from the early 17th century. The rooms to the east were rebuilt after a fire. Ernest and Richenda Matthews lived there. He was a teacher at the Congregational Sunday School. At the end of the lane facing you is 'Willowdale' owned by the Masters family. This was the smallholding to which Bertie Steel, the landlord of the 'Edward VII' retired. To the left of that is 'Bumble Barn' the home of the Pearces, who bred Old English Sheepdogs.

Back on the right hand side of Pound Green is 'Worboys Court', formerly the builders and undertakers yard of John and Albert Worboys. The site was donated by the brothers for houses to be let to people with connections to the village. Next to that is situated the new village school built in 1974 on Back Orchard Meadow. Opposite the school are two cottages once occupied by George and Margaret Webb and Francis and Jessie Webb. End on to the road are three cottages where once lived Cyril and Florence Conder, Elsie Colley and Thomas and Kate Stephenson. John Dellar once lived there with his parents. Peter Turnell also lived there with his parents, Sidney and Mabel. Sidney was killed in Italy in 1944 whilst serving with the Royal Army Medical Corps.

The next building is 'Orchard House', previously a bakery owned by the Rules. It was later occupied by William and Bertha Gentle. Adjacent to that stood 'Orchard Cottage', now demolished, where once lived Charlie and Emma Lawford. The foundations of the house were terminally damaged during the excavations for the sewerage system.

Dubbs Knoll

The houses in the first section of Dubbs Knoll are all more recent until *'Duck Lake Farmhouse'* where Reg and Mabel Tomlin lived (previously occupied by Wilfred Izzard). The farmhouse dates from the early 1800's and is Grade II listed as are the barns that have been converted into dwellings. The timbers are said to have come from the demolished chapel of Redderia (see Chapter 1).

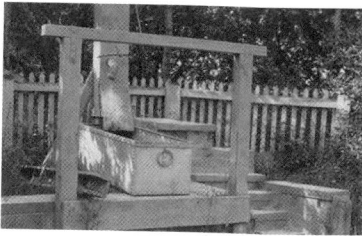

'Chestnut Cottage', where Albert and Alice Conder lived is now demolished and a new house built in its place. Opposite is the village pump, renovated for the Jubilee in 1973. A previous repair was carried out in 1897 when the bill for the work was sent to the Rural District Council. It was reported in 1921 that it was practically impossible to obtain water. Renovation of the pump has again been carried out by village volunteers in 2014, restoring it to its appearance in the photograph above, taken in circa 1925.

Next is a row of cottages called *'Avenel Place'* originally five and now three dwellings. They were once occupied by Alfred Bonfield, Annie Covington, Arthur, Leslie, Thomas and Alma Harris, Olive Waldock, Elizabeth Bonnet and William Covington.[1]

The last house on the left in Dubbs Knoll is *'The Bungalow'* now called *'The Maples'*. Henry Stanley and Ida Rule lived there.

Fox Hill Road

Turning right into Fox Hill Road we find *'Fox Cottage'*, once *'The Fox'* Public House. It dates from the early 17th century with 19th century rebuilding and alteration. It is a Grade II listed building. On the left are all newer houses standing in what was once *'Cannons Meadow'*.

Next is *'Fox Lea'* where Tom and Mona Leonard set up home with John and Marjorie Gentle after their wedding. There is a newer house before the open space called *'The Craft'*.

At the junction of New Road (Kaye's Corner) stands *'Bleak House'* the residence of the blacksmith Oswald Kaye and his wife Ella. He was for many years the Parish Clerk and ran a cycle repair business from this property, the blacksmith's forge

---

[1] The left hand cottage was once occupied by the gymnast and television personality, Suzanne Dando.

being in Church Street. Next to this stand a row of five houses once called *'Phoenix Cottages'* or *'Phoenix Row'* (originally New Road Cottages). The occupants were once Frederick and Edith Bonfield, Oswald and Naomi Dellar, Herbert and Rose Bonfield, Albert and Lizzie Randall and Victor and Winifred Leonard. A weekly doctor's surgery was held at the Leonard's home (see Chapter 5). The rest of the houses are new including those in what was once *'Bells Meadow'* where travelling fairs used to set up.

Opposite Bells Meadow stands the house called *'Six Bells'*, a Grade II listed building. This was once *'The Six Bells'* Public House, run by numerous landlords during the 1940's including Frank Hayward, Alfred Essam, William Brooks, Arthur Brooks, Arthur Bunker and then Fred Blake. It was opened some time before 1801.

On the left at the junction with Church Street are the Village Hall and the Recreation Ground. The eight acres for the recreation ground were bought by the parish in 1912. The village hall was built in 1928 by Arthur Wright and an extension was added in 1949.

Next is the only remaining Public House in the village *'The Edward VII'*, Bertie Steel was the landlord with his wife Alice. Against the wall of this stands a cast iron pump dating from the late 19th century which is Grade II listed. It stands over a well on a cistern. This part of Fox Hill Road was once called Church End.

Church Street

We now enter Church Street with the church on the right. The church dates from the 12th century and is a Grade I listed building. There is more about the church in Chapter 4.

On the left opposite the church were three cottages, some now demolished, whose occupants included Charlie and

Emma Pettengell, Maurice and Mary Rose and John and Edie Izzard. Then a number of other cottages where lived Alfred and Sarah Haylock, Hilda Haylock, Annie Cole, Thomas and Hilda Williams, Mr and Mrs Matthews, Mr and Mrs Stan Clarke, Edward (Teddy) Harris, Frank and Elsie Colley, Gordon and Edith Gentle, Harry and

Winnie Butt, Reg Kirbyshire and James and Hilda Harding. In *'Bear Cottage'* lived John and Rosa Moule and then in the last cottage before Church Lane, Fanny Burr and Flora Wright who was burnt to death in a fire. The Vicarage is next to the Church. The vicars during the 1940s were Llewellyn Price (1919-1945), Allan Gardiner (1945-1949) and David Greenhalgh (1949-1955).

The village sign stands at the entrance to Church Lane and the building behind is the *'Last Forge'*, where once lived Ben (Jack) and Edna Covington and Albert and Emma Kaye. 1970 saw the last of generations of Kayes, who were blacksmiths here. In Church Lane stands *'Dove Cottage'* (formerly a dovecote) which is possibly late 17th or early 18th century, the home of Charlie Pettengell. There is also a well and windlass. Both are Grade II listed.

Further along on the left is the *'Old Post Office'*, a Grade II listed building, dating from the late 17th century with early 19th century additions. Previous shop-keepers were Mrs Jarman then Harry Day and his wife. Between the *'Last Forge'* and the *'Old Post Office'* was a cabbage field in which stood the communal air raid shelter. Beside that are three newer bungalows which stand on the site of the Kaye's Blacksmith's Forge (shown above).

Opposite the *'Old Post Office'* stands *'The Avenels'*, originally home of the owners of *'The Avenels'* Estate, one of the major estates in Guilden Morden. In the 1940's-50's Joseph Hayward and Mr and Mrs Fairchild lived there. Mrs Fairchild was the Red Cross Commandant for the village. Their son was William Fairchild the film director, actor and writer who was married to the actress Isabel Dean.

Following them, Douglas Gordon and his wife lived there. It is a Grade II listed building and originates from around 1681.

Next to *'The Avenels'* is *'Avenel Terrace'* which is comprised of ten[2] two-up two-down dwellings. Originally the toilets were in a barn in the back garden. Previous occupants were Herbert and Queenie Seymour, Charles Worboys, Cyril and Emily Izzard, William and Marjorie Thompson, Kathleen Baulk and Martha Doris Starr, Sarah Holder, Albert and Bessie Webb, Frederick Clark, Harry and Hilda Gentle and Albert Jubber. Opposite *'Avenel Terrace'* is *'Ivy Cottage'* where once lived Florence Churchard and Frances Lilla Kaye, sisters of the blacksmith. It was later owned by William Thompson the postman and his wife Marjorie who served in the shop, parents of Marjorie Baker. They had moved there from *'Avenel Terrace'*. The picture shows *'Sombourne Cottage'* on the left and beyond that *'Avenel Terrace'*. *'Sombourne Cottage'* dates from around 1800 and is a Grade II listed building. Violet, Don and Peggy Mackarsie lived there.

On the opposite side of the road was the old schoolhouse founded originally in 1847. It absorbed the British (chapel) and National (church) schools. This closed in 1974 when the new school opened in Pound Green. Teachers there included Miss Muncey, Miss Kathleen Pullen (Mrs Kershaw), Miss Gabriella Williams, Lelina Williams and Miss Munden. The head teachers lived in the house attached to the school. Further information about the school can be found in Chapter 6.

Nos. 32-34 Church Street, formerly two dwellings, was once occupied by Beatrice and Sarah Annie Levy. The former Dovecote to the rear was the house of Arthur and Dorothy Maud Law. They are both Grade II listed buildings and date from around 1700. They were owned by the Levy family. Next, *'Saville House'* was once a boarding school for about six girls run by Elizabeth Clark. It was later owned by the Saunderson family, millers.

Just before 'Connors Corner' was *'Rose Cottage'* once occupied by Jim and Fanny Worboys and Betty Platt. Next to that stood the tiny cottage, now demolished, occupied in the 40's by Les and Emily Huffer and their daughter Jean.

---

[2] Now consolidated into eight cottages.

Returning to Pound Green at Connors Corner -

Pound Green

This part of Pound Green was once called Towns End. On the left is Swan Lane where stands *'Swan House'*, once *'The Black Swan'* Public House, where Arthur and Edith Crow lived. And down the lane beside that was *'Swan Cottage'* where lived Simeon and Mary Starr.

High Street West and Silver Street

Turning left out of Church Street into the High Street and on the right you come to *'Town Farm House'*. Farmer William Connor lived there with his wife Isabel. The old house (pictured right) has been demolished and replaced by a new one which stands further back.

Further along on the same side is *'The Three Tuns'* Public House, a Grade II listed building dating from the 18th century. The business closed in 2013. The landlords in the 1940's were Bernard Cheslyn followed by John and Emily Gray (nee Cheslyn)

Past the pub is the turning into Silver Street, an old Roman road which continued through Church Lane and across the Recreation Ground to Flecks Lane.

The first house on the right in Silver Street is *'Lodge Farm'*, residence of Herbert and Florence Covington. The big barn was used to store old newspapers for recycling during the war. Next is the cottage of the Lilley family called *'Thatchletts'*, a Grade II listed building of the late 17th or early 18th century. After four new buildings stands the end house, once the home of Joseph and Elizabeth Stenton. Turning back on the other side of the street, opposite the Stentons' house there were one or two houses now demolished. After that there is a pair of cottages occupied by John and Win Godman and Fred and Emma Clements. There are some newer houses before we come to *'Tile Cottage'*, once the dairy of Murfitt's Farm.

Back on the High Street is what was once the shop and cottage of Annie Murfitt (pictures right) known as *'Horse Shoe Cottage'*. As well as sweets and paraffin etc. milk from the dairy in Silver Street was sold. It is a Grade II listed building dating from the early 17th century. Inside can be seen traces of an old bread oven.

Keeping to the west side of the High Street heading south we come to *'Well Cottage'* the home of Martha (Polly) and Mary Long. It is a late 17th or 18th century Grade II listed building. The next house was the home of Bill and Ivy Dellar. This is a Grade II listed building of the late 17th to early 18th century. Bill was an Air Raid Warden, and the house was used for the 'ARP' meetings. It was one of the first houses in the village to have electricity (downstairs only). After one newer house stands the house and Home Farm of Charles and Mary Ann Murfitt. Frank and Jessie Murfitt lived there from 1948. Next to the farm is another house, the home of Norman and Isabel Murfitt (where some ex German prisoners of war lived after the Second World War). This is followed by a bungalow named *'Neasden'*, the home of Thomas and Mary Hyde. Then comes *'Balcarres'* the home of Sidney and Marion Lindsay, the bakers. The house called *'Slapestones'* was previously two cottages called *'The Dene'*, the home of Gordon and Eleanor Grocott and Gladys Worboys. It is a Grade II Listed building of the early 19th century. The thatched cottage that is now 66 High Street was the home of Simeon and Rebecca Dellar. Next to that stands the cottage of Millie Morris where the Mence sisters lived as evacuees.

After some newer houses stands what was *'The Chestnut Tree'* public house, last run by George and Lilian Reynolds. Further along is Granny Cole's house. Mrs Cole was a well known local character who raised eight children and was a 'sergeant' of the local land workers. The picture on the left shows Granny Cole's house with the *'Chestnut Tree'* beyond.

High Street East and Buxtons Lane

Across the road, now heading north, the first house on the east side of the High Street belonged to Frederick and Harriet Skinner. Beside that is *'Jasmine House'* the home of Esther Gordon (this is where Douglas and Peter Wiggett lived as evacuees.)

After a newer house stands *'The Priory'*, (pictured right) the barn of which has been converted into a dwelling. *'The Priory'* is a Grade II listed building dating from the 16th century with late 17th and 19th century alterations and additions. It was once the home of the Berengers and Harold and Enid Griffin.

Next to *'The Priory'* was Ned's Cottage (just visible in the previous picture but now demolished). Behind that was Ned's Pond where the local children used to catch newts. After a newer house is the home of Fred, Lizzie and Phyllis Watts.

Next to this is the *'Old Manse'* home of the Congregational minister, the Rev. Harold Hawkes and his wife Laura. The ministers now live in a new house adjoining the Chapel. After two newer houses is a pair of cottages (once three or four) occupied by Harry Gentle, Mrs Izzard, Jean Huffer and the Mannings .

All the houses in Buxtons Lane on the right are comparatively new apart from the cottage, shown on the right, which was once two or three dwellings. They were occupied by the McConnells and Ted Watts. This was the First Meeting House of the Independent Chapel.

At the junction of Buxtons Lane and the High Street stands the *'Old Bakery'* behind which, in Buxtons Lane, was the Bakery and shop (now demolished) where bread, cakes and pastries could be purchased. The business belonged to George and Winifred Lindsay and later their son Sidney and his wife Marion.

After two newer houses comes *'Robin Dell'* the home of Harry and Margaret Dellar, once *'The Pig and Whistle'* Public House. Harry was a long standing member of the Parish Council, acting as Vice-Chairman for some time.

There are two other new buildings before coming to *'The Cottage'* and adjoining barn, now converted into a dwelling. *'The Cottage'* belonged to Major and Dorothy Aldridge who owned the Nursery which was in the lane beside the barn. This barn was once a slaughter house and before that was used for dances and other functions at about the time of the First World War. Next to *'The Cottage'* stands the disused dairy of Home Farm, after which are three cottages standing end-on to the street, formerly a farmhouse. These are 39, 41 and 43 High Street and are Grade II listed buildings dating from late 17th century with later alterations. They were occupied by Dorothy and Elsie Oliver, Mrs Dellar and Elsie and George Izzard.

Opposite *'The Three Tuns'*, stood a block of four homes called *'Clifden Cottages'*, now demolished. Emma Newell, Hilda Covington, Rupert and Dora Dellar and Alf and Alice Evans lived there. The one shown in the picture was used as the first non-conformist preaching room (once the Dame School).

Potton Road and Little Green

We start at the *'Black Horse'* cottage in Potton Road, a former Public House built in 1888. The landlords were Frank and Kate Bonfield. Their daughter Lilian was married from here in 1941 to Sid Thompson who lived next door in *'Cherry Holt'*. The garden of this property was once on the opposite side of the road and included a well, now part of a new bungalow built on the site. Behind *'The Black Horse'* stands a derelict cottage once lived in by the Scotts.

The next house is a Grade II listed building, late 17th century, called *'Cherry Holt'*. The house was subject to a serious fire in June 2011 when about a third of the thatched roof was destroyed. It was once the home of Sid Thompson.

The large farmhouse next door is *'Grove House'*, the former home of John and Albert Worboys. The brothers were farmers, builders and undertakers. Their legacy to the village is *'Worboys Court'*, the site of their builders and undertakers yard. At the junction to Little Green stands Green Knoll Farm.

Little Green was a hamlet comprising several houses. The only ones remaining are the two cottages on the left and *'Thatchways'* on the right. The two cottages were the homes of Jack and Kate Webb, Les Worboys (a former Japanese prisoner of war), and Harry and Olive Wagg. The site of Sam Stockwell's smallholding, *'Little Green Farm'*, is now occupied by a large new house. *'Thatchways'* is a Grade II listed building dating from the late 17th to early 18th century. It is now a Kennels and Cattery The owner during the 40's and 50's was George Morgan who ran a whiting (sports field marking) business from there.

New Road

The first house on the left in New Road is *'Hillcrest'* the only remaining bungalow of three that originally stood on what was first known as Wendy Road. It was occupied by Herbert and Elizabeth Hart during the 1940's. On the opposite side of the road are six council houses built in 1939. No.1 was occupied by Robert and Elizabeth Merrill, No.2 by Arthur and Winifred Kirbyshire and No.3 by Harry and Joyce Hart. Gordon and Edith Gentle lived in No.4 and in Nos.5 and 6 were Joseph and Priscilla Peckett with their large family. Six new council houses were built next to 'Hillcrest' in the 1940's.

Further along on the same side of the road is the Cemetery, land for which was purchased by the Parish Council and which was opened in 1898. The cemetery was consecrated in 1947. The left hand side is allocated to Church of England burials and the right to the Chapel. A full list of those buried here, along with the plot number, is available on the Guilden Morden Parish website.

Great Green

The second house on the right in Great Green is 'Appletree Cottage' and just behind that, 'Sideways Cottage' the home of Victoria Furley in the 1940's. On the opposite side of the road is Rectory Farm. Alec Jennings and Monte Crittall were the farmers in the 40's. One of the old barns here is a Grade II listed building. It dates from the late 17th century and is timber framed and weather boarded with a corrugated iron roof. On August Bank Holiday 1941 a string of incendiary bombs fell on the farm causing considerable damage. Alec Jennings was the farmer at the time and he made safe two of the bombs that failed to ignite.

Next to Rectory Farm is a lane leading to the site of the Old Brick Works. A new house (built in 1957) stands where there once existed a row of three cottages. Frederick, Ellen, Reg and Arthur Kirbyshire lived here, as did Fred and Margaret Starr. Selina Dellar died here in 1944. She was the widow of John Benjamin Dellar, previously publican of the Edward VII. The only visible evidence of the brickfields is the ponds from which the clay for the bricks was extracted. In 1690, documents mention of 'Brick-kiln Furlong' which was probably related to this site. The brickworks were disused by the 1930's.

Next is 'Peartree Cottage', once 'The Peartree' Public House, the home of James and Emily Woods. This is a Grade II listed building. Then comes Valley Farm where lived Fred and Sarah Dennis, later their son Maurice and his wife Phyllis (nee Huffer). 'Valley Farmhouse' is a Grade II listed building, late 17th to early 18th century with 19th and 20th century alterations and renovation.

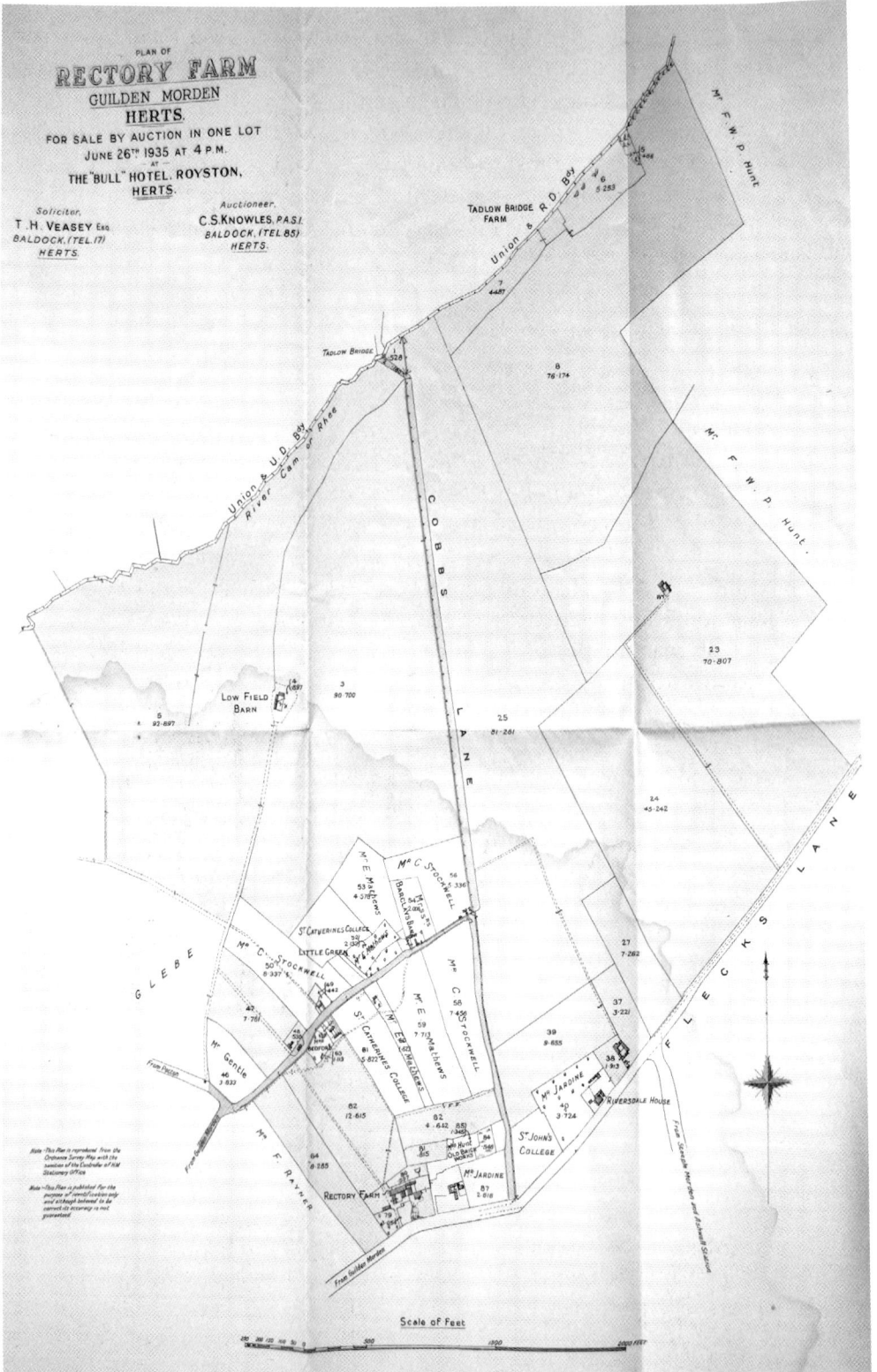

PLAN OF
RECTORY FARM
GUILDEN MORDEN
HERTS.
FOR SALE BY AUCTION IN ONE LOT
JUNE 26TH 1935 AT 4 P.M.
AT
THE "BULL" HOTEL. ROYSTON,
HERTS.

Solicitor,
T.H. VEASEY Esq.
BALDOCK, (TEL.17)
HERTS.

Auctioneer.
C.S.KNOWLES, P.A.S.I.
BALDOCK, (TEL.85)
HERTS.

Scale of Feet

Opposite *'The Peartree'* is the drive leading to the smallholding called *'Killarney'*. In November 1941 William James Gentle of *'Orchard House'*, Guilden Morden, married Elsie Hilda Rayner daughter of the late Mr and Mrs Frederick Rayner of *'Killarney'* and they set up home here.

Back to the other side of the road and after a newer house is a lane called The Slipe which forms part of the eastern boundary of Guilden Morden Parish. It is a section of Cobbs Lane, which ran from Tadlow to Odsey. In the 1940's there were two or three cottages here of which no trace remains. George Hurrell, John Webb and Percy and Hannah Worboys lived there.

Some other places of interest

Hooks Mill

Hooks Mill lies in the northern-most part of Guilden Morden parish, fed by a leat from the River Cam or Rhee. There has been a mill on this site for many years: it is almost certainly the site of a mill belonging to Picot mentioned in the Doomsday Book. Documentary sources indicate that it was in continuous use until 1935 when it ceased operation. The last miller was Ernest Carter. The main source of the river is the springhead in Ashwell, although it is also fed by smaller brooks from West End, Ashwell and Ruddery Spring in Guilden Morden.

The present road to the mill from Guilden Morden was already in existence at the time of enclosure in 1804. At this time, the course of the road northwards between the mill and Tadlow was altered and straightened. Other than a footpath from Little Green which joins the main road a few yards south of the entry to the mill, there appears to have been no other communication between the mill and the settlement.
Source: Maurice Hempsel.

The names of some of the millers were as follows:

William Hoppot	c1778
Thomas Quinton	c1804
Nathaniel Barker	c1847-1851
Thomas Dickason	c1853-1858
George Sanderson	c1864
George Aaron Sanderson	c1869-1892
Alfred Sanderson	c1896-1919
Arthur Sanderson	c1919 (bought by a Mr Huckle)
William Carter	c1919
Ernest Carter	c1933-1935, when it was closed.

A brief memoir from Miss Mary Carter, born 1924, daughter of Ernie Carter
(as related to a member of the History Group)
Mary lived at Hooks Mills all her life until she moved to a Care Home in 2008. Her father acquired the farm in 1919. It lies about ¾ mile from the village.

She remembers walking or cycling to the village school with her sisters. Sometimes her father drove them up Potton Road to 'The Black Horse' and they linked up with the Bonfield family and walked on from there together. They took packed lunches.

She left school at fourteen in 1938 and kept house, with her mother, on their farm. Her sister Megan, born 1928, worked the farm with her father Ernest Carter. Her younger sister Maureen, born 1930, won a scholarship place in 1945 to Secondary School and eventually did City and Guilds Examinations and worked outside the village.

Megan and Maureen are in the front row in the 1940 school photograph (see Chapter 6). They both learned to drive. Mary cycled. She continued cycling regularly to the village church until she was nearly seventy five.

Her father, Ernest, was keen on motoring and upgraded his vehicle whenever possible. Mary remembers his motorbike and sidecar. At one time he was a Church Warden.

She never saw the steam watermill in operation but the windmill was in operation during her childhood.

During the war they had Italian POW's who were *"really nice boys and very respectful. Father was pleased about that"*. When they left they gave her a small alabaster figure of the Virgin Mary and two white alabaster doves. Mary used these for seasonal decorations in church.

Mary enjoyed having animals around the farm especially the pet donkeys and chickens. She was a renowned cake maker for church and village events and a faithful worshipper at St Mary's Church, where she enjoyed large scale flower arranging. Piano playing was a hobby she took up later in life.

Morden Hall

The Hall has medieval origins and is completely surrounded by its own moat, well stocked with rudd and carp.

In the early part of the twelfth century the property belonged to Pain Peverel of Dover but when his son, William, died without issue the land around Guilden Morden was divided into five estates and shared between his sisters. Some of these estates were later acquired by the Crown under Edward I. Others remained in private ownership passing through the generations. In 1346 Sir William Lovell became owner of Morden Hall following his marriage to Margaret Hereward, but he died in 1348 after mortally wounding his steward in his own hall and fleeing Guilden Morden. The original hall was

destroyed in the Peasants Revolt of 1381 by which time it was owned by Thomas Haselden. He was a Yorkshireman who arrived in Cambridgeshire as steward to John of Gaunt in 1370 and was controller of his household from 1372 to 1382. Morden Hall remained in the Haselden family and was largely rebuilt during the fifteenth century.

The Morden manors (including Morden Hall) were sold in 1615 to William Hayes. William died in 1617 and ownership passed to his nephew Thomas who in turn died in 1628. Ownership then passed to Thomas's son William who was then aged two, although it seems likely that the estate was then occupied by his father's creditors. William recovered possession in about 1647 until his death in 1651. His widow married Thomas Storey and ownership passed in 1675 to their son Thomas. It was on his death in 1702 that the estate was sold to pay his debts.

The estate was eventually purchased in 1667 by Sir George Downing - Secretary of the UK Treasury[3] and grandfather of the founder of Downing college, Cambridge. In 1806 it was sold to Lord Hardwicke and remained with the Hardwicke's Wimpole Estate until the early part of this century. In 1911, part of the estate, including Morden Hall, was purchased by Cambridge County Council and remained in their ownership until the early 1980's.
Source: www.mordenhall.co.uk

Odsey

'The name Odsey survives in Odsey Grange and manor in the parish of Guilden Morden, Cambs. The Grange now lies without the county boundary, but in the first half of the 16th century the lands of the manor extended into Hertfordshire and Speed's map of the county published in 1611 shows Odsey Grange within the county boundary and in the hundred of Odsey....'
Source: Victoria County History

'The Manor, or Grange, of Odsey gives its name to one of the Hundreds of Hertfordshire, which includes sixteen parishes and about 31,000 acres. Odsey itself lies along the Icknield Way on the west side and is now partly in Cambridgeshire. It was never a separate parish. Some trace of Romano-British settlement is recorded in a paper read by Sir George Fordham before the Cambridge Antiquarian Society about 1900.

That Odsey House (shown right) was built between 1722 and 1729 is fixed by deeds which recite that *'the said mansion, or Great House, Jockey House, Stables and buildings ..... were erected or built by William the second Duke of Devonshire'*. In all probability the house was built in 1723. The fine proportions of the Court Yard, the

---

[3] Downing Street, the official home of the Prime Minister, was named in honour of Sir George Downing

classic details of the panelling, the acanthus frieze and fir cones on the corners of the drawing-room cornice over the fireplace suggest the work of William Kent who built Devonshire House in 1733, and also the Horse Guards and many London houses.....

In September 1793 the Fifth Duke of Devonshire (husband of Georgiana Spencer) sold the Odsey Estate to George Fordham of Sandon Bury and Edward King Fordham of Royston, banker, for the sum of £3600.....'

Source: Notes made by Ernest O Fordham of Odsey House, which were published in the Mordens Women's Institute scrapbook of 1957.

Origin of the name of Odsey

'The name is older than the Hundred it represents and through the centuries has been spelt in such various ways as Odeseie, Odesey, Odesheis, Oddes(h)eye, Odeseth(e), Oddeseth(e). But since it lies in a hollow on the Icknield Way, with both a gravel pit and an old chalk pit nearby, it probably derives from Odda's hollow or pit.

The coming of the railway in 1850 was a big event for Odsey. The station, known as Ashwell and Morden, was a very busy place from the time of the coprolite digging until road transport began to take traffic from the railways in recent years.

The Mill Room, where the coprolites were brought to be washed and ground, has since the end of the trade, been used as a place of worship and as a dwelling house. At one time the Odsey Women's Institute held their meetings there.

The Railway Tavern[4], according to old maps, was originally known as the Traveller's Rest. For licensing purposes there is still a 'Petty Division of Odsey....'

Source: The Mordens Women's Institute Scrapbook of 1957

---

[4] Now 'The Jester'.